CHILDREN'S MENTAL HEALTH RESOURCES FOR THE CHURCH

DAWN M. DOERR-JOHNSON

Judson Press™
DISTINGUISHED PUBLISHERS SINCE 1824
VALLEY FORGE, PA

Children's Mental Health Resources for the Church

Interior design by Crystal Devine.
Cover design by Lisa Cain.
Author photo on back cover taken by Wise Owl Multimedia.

Library of Congress Control Number: 2025945053

Printed in the U.S.A.

First printing, 2025.

CONTENTS

INTRODUCTION

Jesus loves the little children,
All the children of the world.
He sees us each as truly whole
And cares for every unique soul.
Jesus loves the little children of the world!

Many people turn to the church in their time of crisis. For many, now is that time of crisis. In this country, we have a mental health crisis for children. Since before the COVID quarantine, we have seen increasing rates of diagnoses while also experiencing a shortage of providers for a myriad of reasons.[1] The church can fill part of this need caused by the lack of providers, which would answer the church's call to go beyond support to healing. Behavioral Health Intervention Services (BHIS) can benefit children between the ages of four and eighteen facing mental health challenges. The teaching of coping, communication, anger management, and social skills has long been part of the hidden curriculum of Sunday school and Vacation Bible School. Now is the time to come out of the dark and address these services directly. By providing these church leaders with more training, they can become part of the solution. This book provides some of that training.

Fathers, do not provoke your children to anger, but bring them up in the discipline and instruction of the Lord. (EPHESIANS 6:4)

Introduction to Behavioral Health

Here are a few facts regarding the state of children and youth mental health in the United States:

- ADHD, anxiety problems, behavior problems, and depression are the most diagnosed mental disorders in children.
- One in six US children aged two to eight years (17.4 percent) had a diagnosed mental, behavioral, or developmental disorder.
- Among adolescents, 18.8 percent seriously considered attempting suicide.
- Among children living below the federal poverty level, more than one in five (22 percent) had a mental, behavioral, or developmental disorder.[2]

Behavioral health interventions focus on teaching social skills, stress management, self-esteem, and other important skills. These skills influence a child's success in school and in life. Serious or persistent difficulty in reaching milestones or coping with stressors may lead to a mental health diagnosis now or later.

While only a licensed professional can determine the need for behavioral therapy, the treatment can be administered and supported by others. Treatment is most successful when it is conducted in collaboration between the professional who diagnoses and provides therapy to address the question of *why* there is a problem and other providers who address the question of *how* the problem can be dealt with.

A church that feels called to address the mental health crisis needs to have a licensed professional in its program. This can be an LMFT (Licensed Marriage and Family Therapist), LMHC (Licensed Mental Health Counselor), LISW (Licensed Independent Social Worker), or any of several other licenses qualified to diagnose mental health problems. The program can hire this person or, optionally, may be able to attach itself to an outside mental health practice as a provider to that practice's clients.

The church that brings in a clinician maintains control of the program and may choose to provide services at a nominal or no fee. With a little work on accreditation, they could even accept Medicaid reimbursement. They can set their policies and procedures. The churches that attach themselves to an established practice may forego a lot of administrative hassle.

BHIS changes problem behaviors by building skills and helping their clients to learn to manage their behaviors. Family sessions help build parenting skills and the relationships between parents and children. It keeps kids in their homes and schools as opposed to residential treatment. These intensive skill-based services impact the success of children and youth at home, at school, and in the community. They improve the youth's self-control and ability to manage their behaviors.

Areas of Need

Sometimes, a child's area of need coincides with their diagnosis, but not always. Do not confuse the two. As a BHIS provider, your program will address the child's area of need. Maybe the child is anxious with a generalized anxiety diagnosis. Perhaps, though, their anxiety is a result of obsessions. Their diagnosis may be helpful, but you are addressing their *need*.

Common Behavior Health Terms

Anxiety disorders include excessive fear and anxiety and related behaviors. Fear is a response to a real or perceived threat, while anxiety is the anticipation of a reaction. They are different from developmentally appropriate fear or anxiety.[3]

Depression is the presence of a sad, empty, or irritable mood, accompanied by physical and cognitive changes. These symptoms are present in multiple diagnoses.[4]

Social skills, sometimes called soft skills, include the ability to choose and interpret appropriate verbal and nonverbal communications.[5] The absence or degradation of social skills can aggravate the distress of individuals with mental health needs, as it interferes with the support networks they need to overcome challenges.[6]

Coping skills include helpful thoughts and behaviors for navigating stressful situations.[7] Everyone develops skills to cope with the problems in their life. We want individuals to use healthy coping skills rather than unhealthy ones like meltdowns, infantile behavior, and substance use.[8]

Self-esteem, including self-confidence or feeling good about yourself, is important to good mental health. It is built with real success in attempted activities.[9]

Communication skills involve sending and receiving information and understanding. Note: it is not just the sending or receiving but includes understanding.[10]

Anger management includes skills for directing anger appropriately. Everyone gets angry. It is not wrong to be angry, but we want clients to manage their reactions in positive ways.

Goal-setting is an important part of becoming successful. This skill involves understanding what you want and having a socially appropriate plan to achieve it.[11]

Program Specifics

This book is not designed for creating a specific program. You will not find program specifics in this book. I will not tell you to meet on Wednesdays for three hours and serve supper. You know your community and its needs better than a stranger. This book strives to provide a general overview of a program that needs to be highly individualized to the community and to the individual being provided help. It is most effective to have a high adult-to-child ratio—1:1 is best—and to meet with the child for at least one hour a week, along with additional meetings with the family.

Questions for Reflection and Discussion

How did you become interested in the field of mental health as a church? As an individual?
What strengths do you bring to this work?
What do you need to learn to do this work?
What experience do you have working with children from age three to young adults, age twenty?

NOTES

1. Lindsey Phillips "A Closer Look at the Mental Health Provider Shortage," *Counseling Today*, May 2023. Accessed May 27, 2025.
2. Data and Statistics on Children's Mental Health, Centers for Disease Control, March 13, 2023, https://www.cdc.gov/children-mental-health/data-research/?CDC_AAref_Val=https://www.cdc.gov/childrensmentalhealth/data.html.
3. Brenda W. J. H. Penninx, et al., "Anxiety disorders," *Lancet,* 2021 Mar 6; 397(10277): 914–927.
4. Suma P. Chand and Hasan Arif, "Depression," [Updated 2023 Jul 17]. In: StatPearls [Internet]. Treasure Island, FL: StatPearls Publishing; 2025. Available from: https://www.ncbi.nlm.nih.gov/books/NBK430847/.
5. Social Skills, APA Dictionary, retrieved June 10, 2025, https://dictionary.apa.org/social-skills.
6. Lasse Brandt, et al., "The effects of social isolation stress and discrimination on mental health," *Translational Psychiatry*, 2022 Sep 21; 12(1):398.
7. Emad B. Algorani and Vikas Gupta, "Coping Mechanisms," StatPearls, April 24, 2023, National Library of Medicine, accessed June 10, 2025, https://www.ncbi.nlm.nih.gov/books/NBK559031/.
8. Agus Setiawan, et al., "Coping Mechanisms Utilized by Individuals With Drug Addiction in Overcoming Challenges During the Recovery Process: A Qualitative Meta-synthesis," *Journal of Preventive Medicine and Public Health*. 2024 May; 57(3):197-211.
9. Agus Setiawan et al., 197–211.
10. Communication Skills. https://www.skillsyouneed.com/ips/communication-skills.html.
11. Matthew Hughes Personal Goal-Setting. https://www.mindtools.com/a5ykiuq/personal-goal-setting?from=shared-link.

CHAPTER ONE

AGES AND STAGES

As professionals in the relationship, we often need to remind ourselves and the parents of our clients what a child is capable of. Sometimes we expect too much, and other times we expect too little. It helps to have familiarity with the major theories of child development.

Children develop in a pattern, and many theorists would be happy to tell you what to expect when. Unfortunately, there is disagreement among them. This chapter will provide a short overview of what to expect and when a behavior is not within the normal parameters expected of a child of that age or stage.

We also find our first case study here. Case studies summarize the important points in a case to prompt thinking about the issues and learning from them. In a case study, we learn of the child's background, history, treatment, needs, and goals.

Lucy

Name: Lucy
Age: 18
Gender: Female
Ethnicity: White
School: Blossom GIRLS program (GIRLS programs are gender-based programs that include educational and

mental health services outside of a school or hospital setting. This one stands for Girls In Remedial Learning Situations. They are designed to address specific gender needs and are becoming rare due to changes in funding structures. They often operate within the school district as a separate program where the clients are enrolled in the host district or their original district.)

Health: Genital-urinary complications of abuse

Family Members: Sarah, mother, non-custodial; Gary, father with termination of parental rights

Relationship Status: None

Family Health History: None noted

Alcohol/Drug Use: None reported

Challenges: Survivor of childhood sexual abuse, non-custodial parents

Goals: Graduate from high school, have a boyfriend and a baby

Coping Skills: Sense grounding, deep breathing

Strengths: Compassion, strong narrative skills (telling stories)

Weaknesses: Dissociates under stress, low math skills, urinary issues, anger management problems, relationship deficits

Symptoms/Problems: Effects of childhood abuse on relationships, emotional stability problems, nightmares, flashbacks

Diagnosis: Complex PTSD (Post Traumatic Stress Disorder)

Treatment Goals/Progress: Reduce frequency and duration of dissociation by 25 percent in twelve months; reduce suicidal ideation by 25 percent with no attempts in six months; improve relationship skills as evidenced by three relationships of three months' duration within twelve months

Case Conceptualization and Discussion

DEVELOPMENTAL NEEDS

Lucy was a fourteen-year-old female. She resided in a succession of foster homes of varying quality. At the age of two, she was placed in her father's care when her mother stated she could not care for the child. The arrangement was informal with no involvement by the state. While in her father's care, the child was sold or given to adult men in exchange for drugs or to pay debts. This time in a child's life is important according to developmental specialists because, according to prominent child psychoanalyst Erik Erikson, they are developing toward autonomy or shame and doubt.[1] Personal control is the key at this stage.

By the time she was three, she had sustained injuries from abuse that led to her spending three months in the hospital. During this time, her mother was convinced to regain custody and her father's parental rights were terminated. This arrangement lasted almost a year before Mom gave her up again and she was placed in foster care. Throughout her childhood and teen years, she would return to her mother and then return to foster care numerous times. When asked to terminate her mother's rights so that she could be adopted, the court declined, stating that her chances of adoption as a teen were small.

During her teen years, the young woman was self-abusive and often suicidal. She dealt with periods of dissociation. Continuing into adulthood, she was sexually promiscuous and often reported that she was pregnant, despite the former abuse making her chances of pregnancy low. She suffered from an explosive temper when her feelings became overwhelming.

Lucy completed a curriculum on sexual abuse. In it, trusted adults told her repeatedly that she was not at fault for her abuse. She was instructed in ways that changed the way she looked at things. Despite this instruction, caregivers could not tolerate her rages. She was taught grounding skills when she dissociated and employed them to return to the present. Lucy stopped abusing herself sexually but continued to engage in risky sex. Lucy's best chance is to develop higher self-esteem and to build lasting, unconditional relationships.

But grow in the grace and knowledge of our Lord and Savior Jesus Christ. To him be the glory both now and to the day of eternity. Amen. (2 PETER 3:18)

Lucy's case is important because we can follow her through the developmental stages and see where things went wrong and why she has responded as she has. She experienced major attachment injuries at important times in her life, and noting when these injuries occurred helps her behaviors make sense.

Lucy could have benefited from a caring church and still can. She needs consistent role models. She needs friends with a positive outlook. She cannot be told of her value too often. Children in a BHIS program may choose to maintain relationships with their providers far into adulthood as they seek that consistency.

Major Theories about Children's Development

JEAN PIAGET

The first theorist we examine is the noted psychologist Jean Piaget. Piaget identified four major developmental stages. Note that in Piaget's theory, the age at which the stage is reached is not as important as understanding that they always follow this order. Think back to the case study. Why is Lucy's age at which the break in trust with her father occurred important?

SENSORIMOTOR

(Birth through ages eighteen to twenty-four months)

Your clients are likely to have passed this stage before they are eligible for BHIS services, but some may still be here or be back here because of injury or disease. Children in this stage focus on what they see, what they are doing, and physical interactions with their immediate environment. Because they do not yet know how things react, they constantly experiment. This is why babies put everything in their mouths.

PREOPERATIONAL

(Toddlerhood, from around eighteen to twenty-four months through early childhood, typically age seven)

During this stage, young children can think symbolically. Their language use becomes more mature. They also develop memory and imagination, allowing them to understand the difference between past and future and engage in make-believe. Their thinking is based on intuition and is still not completely logical. They cannot yet grasp more complex concepts such as cause and effect, time, and comparison. These clients may not respond to punishment or correction if it is not offered at the time of the infraction.

CONCRETE OPERATIONAL

(Ages seven to twelve)

Most of your clients will fall into this stage of development. Indeed, their problems may stem from higher expectations than they can achieve. Children's thinking becomes less egocentric, and they are increasingly aware of external events. They begin to realize that one's thoughts and feelings are unique and may not be shared by others or be part of reality.

FORMAL OPERATIONAL

(Adolescence through adulthood)

Adolescents who reach this fourth stage of intellectual development (usually at age eleven) can logically use symbols related to abstract concepts, such as algebra and science. They can think about multiple variables in systematic ways, formulate hypotheses, and consider possibilities. They also can ponder abstract relationships and concepts such as justice.[2]

❋ ERIK ERIKSON

Our next theorist is Erik Erikson. His theory revolves around experiences of a psychosocial crisis, which could have a positive or negative outcome on personality development. Each stage presents a different crisis, the response to which shapes personality development. Only the first five affect your typical BHIS client. Again, consider the case study. What significant events happened in the first stage of Lucy's life due to her developmental stage?

1. TRUST VERSUS MISTRUST

Trust versus mistrust is the first stage in Erik Erikson's theory of psychosocial development. This stage begins at birth and continues until approximately eighteen months of age. During this stage, the infant is uncertain about the world in which they live and looks toward their primary caregiver for stability and consistency of care. Problems in this stage can lead to attachment problems, which you will see later in life.

2. AUTONOMY VERSUS SHAME AND DOUBT

This stage occurs between the ages of eighteen months to approximately three years. While this stage happens before they come to you, it will still affect them. According to Erikson, children at this stage are focused on developing a sense of personal control over physical skills and a sense of independence. Erikson states it is critical that parents allow their children to explore the limits of their abilities within an encouraging environment tolerant of failure.

3. INITIATIVE VERSUS GUILT

Initiative versus guilt is the third stage of Erikson's theory of psychosocial development and occurs approximately at 4–5 years in age. During the initiative versus guilt stage, children assert themselves more frequently. Children begin to plan activities, make up games, and initiate activities with others. If given this opportunity, children develop a sense of initiative and feel secure in their ability to lead others and make decisions. At this stage, the child will begin to ask many questions as his thirst for knowledge grows. If the parents treat the child's questions as trivial, annoying, or embarrassing, or other aspects of their behavior as threatening, then the child may have feelings of guilt for being a nuisance.

4. INDUSTRY VERSUS INFERIORITY

Erikson's fourth psychosocial crisis, involving industry (competence) versus inferiority, occurs between the ages of five and twelve. Teachers begin to play an important role in the child's life as they teach the child specific skills.

At this stage, the child's peer group will gain greater significance and will become a major source of the child's self-esteem. If children are encouraged and reinforced for their initiative, they begin to feel industrious (competent) and confident in their ability to achieve goals. If this initiative is not encouraged or if parents or teachers restrict it, then children begin to feel inferior, doubt their abilities, and therefore may not reach their potential. A balance between competence and modesty is necessary.[3]

5. IDENTITY VERSUS ROLE CONFUSION

Erikson's fifth stage of psychosocial development is identity versus role confusion, and it occurs during adolescence, from ages twelve to eighteen. During this stage, adolescents search for a sense of self and personal identity through an intense exploration of personal values, beliefs, and goals. During this stage, adolescents reexamine their identities and try to discover who they are. Erikson suggests that sexual and occupational identities are involved.

What should happen at the end of this stage is "a reintegrated sense of self, of what one wants to do or be, and of one's appropriate sex role."[4] During this stage, the body image of the adolescent changes. Fidelity involves committing oneself to others based on accepting others, even when there may be ideological differences. In response to role confusion or identity crisis, an adolescent may begin to experiment with different lifestyles (e.g., work, education, or political activities).

LAWRENCE KOHLBERG

American psychologist Lawrence Kohlberg is our third theorist, known for his work on moral development. These six levels are not age-based, but like Piaget's, they always follow this order. Understanding a client's stage (or their parents') can clarify motivation and choosing effective discipline.

LEVEL 1: PRECONVENTIONAL

Throughout the preconventional level, a child's sense of morality is externally controlled. Children accept and believe the rules of authority figures such as parents and teachers.

The first stage of the preconventional level is Obedience and Punishment Orientation, which focuses on the child's desire to obey rules and avoid punishment. The second stage is called Instrumental Orientation. Children in this orientation express the "What's in it for me?" position, in which the right behavior is defined by whatever the individual believes to be in their best interest.

LEVEL 2: CONVENTIONAL

Throughout the conventional level, a child's sense of morality is tied to personal and societal relationships. Children continue to accept the rules of authority figures, but this is now due to their belief that this is necessary to ensure positive relationships and societal order. Adherence to rules and conventions is somewhat rigid during these stages, and a rule's appropriateness or fairness is seldom questioned. This level has two stages.

The third stage, part of the conventional level, is described as the Good Boy, Nice Girl Orientation. In this stage, children want the approval of others and act in ways to avoid disapproval.

The fourth stage is known as the Law and Order Orientation. Children in this stage blindly accept rules and conventions because of their importance in maintaining a functioning society. Rules are seen as the same for everyone and obeying rules by doing what one is "supposed" to do is seen as valuable and important.

LEVEL 3: POSTCONVENTIONAL

Throughout the postconventional level, a person's sense of morality is defined in terms of more abstract principles and values, and they view rules as useful but changeable mechanisms rather than absolute dictates that must be obeyed without question. Some theorists have speculated that many people may never reach this level of abstract moral reasoning. Like the others, this level has two stages.

Kohlberg describes the fifth stage as the Social Contract Orientation. In this stage, the world is viewed as holding different opinions, rights, and values. Such perspectives should be mutually respected as unique to each person or community. Laws are regarded as social contracts rather than rigid edicts.

The Universal Ethical Principles Orientation is the sixth stage. People entering this stage have moral reasoning based on abstract reasoning using universal ethical principles. Generally, the chosen principles are abstract rather than concrete and focus on ideas such as equality, dignity, or respect. Laws are valid only insofar as they are grounded in justice, and a commitment to justice carries with it an obligation to disobey unjust laws. Although Kohlberg insisted that stage six exists, he found it difficult to identify individuals who consistently operated at that level.[5]

Each developmental theorist can tell us something important about our clients' lives. As you develop your program, you may find it helpful to revisit these theorists when thinking about what you are observing.

* * * Appropriate Behavior Can Be Delayed by Trauma[6] * * *

The most important point to learn from this chapter is that development and behavior can be delayed by trauma. Recalling the case study that opened this chapter, Lucy has had more than her fair share of trauma. When she behaves like a two-year-old in the body of a sixteen-year-old, look at what happened to her at the age of two. She was without parents or any adults who would protect her. At an age when she needed it most, this critical aspect of her life was missing, and her mind and body took her back to that time so she could work through it by obtaining what she needed then.

In John 3:4, Nicodemus, asking about spiritual rebirth, asked Jesus, "How can a man be born when he is old? Can he enter a second time into his mother's womb and be born?" Lucy needs a developmental rebirth that the church can point her toward and can provide the structural support to make it happen. As a BHIS provider, knowing what is appropriate and finding the deficits is the ground level of our work.

Questions for Reflection and Discussion

Pat is ten years old and in third grade. The client has an IEP for mathematics and behaviors. Pat lives in an apartment with their mother, grandmother, and toddler sister. Teachers say Pat has few or no friends.

At school this week, Pat got into trouble when they took the new basketball a classmate was playing with to look at it and then flew into a rage, screaming and hitting when the classmate demanded it back. The teacher quickly diffused the situation but was concerned that the client has no empathy for others and cannot control their emotions.

What developmental stage is the client in according to each theorist? What evidence supports your decision?

NOTES

1. Barbara M. Newman and Philip R. Newman, *Development Through Life: A Psychosocial Approach* (Wadsworth Cengage Learning, 2012), 223ff.
2. Rick Ansorge, et al., "Piaget Cognitive Stages of Development," WebMD, https://www.webmd.com/children/piaget-stages-of-development.
3. Saul McLeod, "Erik Erikson's Stages of Psychosocial Development," Simple-Psychology, updated April 18, 2025, https://www.simplypsychology.org/erik-erikson.html.
4. Helen Bee, *The Developing Child* (Harper Collins, 1992), 245.
5. Saul McLeod, "Kohlberg's Stages of Moral Development," SimplyPsychology, updated March 12, 2025, https://www.simplypsychology.org/kohlberg.html.
6. The National Child Traumatic Stress Network, "Effects," https://www.nctsn.org/what-is-child-trauma/trauma-types/complex-trauma/effects.

CHAPTER TWO

COMMON CHILDHOOD DIAGNOSES

Carrie

Name: Carrie
Age: 12
Gender: Female
Ethnicity: White
School: Online public school
Health: Ehlers-Danlos Syndrome (EDS) with hypermobility in the joints, skin is fragile, muscle/joint pain, extreme fatigue, bruises easily (EDS is a hereditary connective tissue disorder with many symptoms beyond those of Carrie. Her mother has it as well but with different symptoms.)
Family Members: Lois, mom, single; Larry, dad, single; Ryan, seventeen-year-old half-brother; Jill, twenty-six-year-old half-sister
Relationship: None
Family Health History: Mom has EDS, as well as depression/anxiety; Dad has likely mental health issues
Alcohol/Drug Use: None
Challenges: Physical challenges due to EDS, extreme social anxiety, homeschooled
Goals: Client can list no goals; Mom's goals for daughter are to graduate from high school and "be a successful adult"
Coping Skills: Drawing, isolation

Strengths: Gifted artist, sense of humor
Weaknesses: Low motivation to change, physical disabilities (hidden)
Symptoms/Problems: Isolates socially, low motivation to address issues, sensory avoiding
Diagnosis: Autism Spectrum Disorder (ASD)
Treatment Goals/Progress:
Develop three relationships outside of family within six months; one must be in real life
Complete the required classes with a passing grade in all
Reduce executive functioning deficits by creating an organizational system for studying by the end of three months

Case Conceptualization and Discussion:

CHANGING DIAGNOSES

Carrie is a twelve-year-old female in shared custody between her mother and her father. Mom is single and has custody of Carrie and her seventeen-year-old brother Ryan from a different father. The mother maintains a rental home and works in education. She also provides respite care for children. Her father owns his home and is self-employed, working in technology from his home. He has another daughter, who is twenty-six years old and lives with her boyfriend in a nearby community.

Carrie has been in therapy since her parents divorced while she was in kindergarten. She has trouble dealing with people and was originally diagnosed with social anxiety. Carrie explains she doesn't understand why people behave the way they do. This anxiety leads to physical symptoms such as headaches and stomachaches. Her father is autocratic, allowing little room for the young woman to mature and develop positive self-worth. Carrie has an uncertain sense of herself and cannot list strengths beyond being artistic. She is an accomplished artist but cannot show her work or interact with the public, constraining the possibility of turning art into a career.

After six years of treating Carrie, her therapist recognized that Carrie's issues were not just social anxiety but high-functioning autism. The best practice for treating autism is usually a behavioral management system, but these are not always used with high-functioning individuals. This idea of a behavioral management system conflicts with Mom's discipline style. Dad doesn't "believe" in therapy.

Carrie has learned how individuals on the spectrum see the world differently, and she sees herself in these descriptions. She has no desire to grow up and has little vision for her future. She is realistic about her limitations but is not motivated to overcome them. Most autism curricula are designed for those lower on the functioning scale, so they are inappropriate for Carrie. Her therapist utilizes art therapy to help Carrie believe in her strengths and encourage her to think beyond the present.

Many of the symptoms of each diagnosis may be seen in other diagnoses as well. Carrie's change in diagnosis is not uncommon. What looked like simple social anxiety changes when more is known. Children cannot give us all the information that we need. Sometimes they do not know what is important. Other times, they simply lack the language to explain until their language skills mature. If a child has a church home, more adult eyes are on them, and more people can report symptoms.

No temptation has overtaken you that is not common to man. God is faithful, and he will not let you be tempted beyond your ability, but with the temptation he will also provide the way of escape, that you may be able to endure it. (1 CORINTHIANS 10:13)

Carrie tends to self-isolate because she does not understand how "normal" people react and has too much history with people who will not tolerate the neurodiverse. The church should be a haven for everyone, even those who do not talk like "us," dress like "us," or think like "us." In the kingdom of God, what we share is more important than our differences.

Common Childhood Diagnoses Seen by BHIS

The BHIS provider is a provider of training and support. Sometimes, you may be the only mental health provider who regularly sees the client. Sometimes, you are the one that parents can reach out to when they do not understand what is going on. As a mental health provider, you serve clients with support they do not get in other places. As such, it is important to understand that people may be carrying multiple physical and mental health challenges, as well as how multiple diagnoses may interact with each other.

A chapter in the 2014 *Handbook of Youth Mentoring* noted that, theoretically, mentors for youth with mental health needs may be helpful in four broad areas.[1] BHIS also provides benefits in these areas:

- Providing support for treatment initiation, adherence, and destigmatization. Caring adult relationships may help youth feel better about their struggles and encourage acceptance of other treatments and services.
- Addressing internalizing problems, such as handling stress and teaching coping strategies.
- Addressing externalizing problems by role modeling effective strategies for living with mental health issues, as well as by monitoring youth to keep them safe, ensuring their forward progress in treatment.
- Addressing suicidality, specifically, by helping youth feel valued, cared for, and emotionally close to a caring adult.

Church members in general and BHIS providers specifically see things that parents and teachers may not. You can provide clues to the licensed provider that can distinguish between one diagnosis and another. Some diagnoses are discussed here.

TRAUMA

Childhood trauma is more common than we might be comfortable with. In fact, over two-thirds of children have experienced a traumatic event by the time they are sixteen, including:

Psychological, physical, or sexual abuse
Community or school violence
Witnessing or experiencing domestic violence
Natural disasters or terrorism
Commercial sexual exploitation
Sudden or violent loss of a loved one
Refugee or war experiences
Military family-related stressors (e.g., deployment, parental loss or injury)
Physical or sexual assault
Neglect
Serious accidents
Life-threatening illness

Signs of trauma differ by age. Be aware of these signs in your clients.

PRESCHOOL CHILDREN

Fear of separation from parent/caregiver
Excessive crying/screaming
Poor eating/losing weight
Nightmares

ELEMENTARY CHILDREN

Anxiety, fearfulness

Guilt or shame
Difficulty concentrating
Difficulty sleeping

MIDDLE SCHOOL OR HIGH SCHOOL CHILDREN

Depression, loneliness
Eating disorders
Self-harm
Substance use/abuse
Risky sexual behaviors[2]

IMPACT OF TRAUMA

The impact of childhood trauma can last beyond the years of childhood. Victims of childhood trauma may experience:

Learning problems, including lower grades and more suspensions and expulsions
Increased use of health and mental health services
Increased involvement with child welfare and juvenile justice systems
Long-term health problems

Critical to recovery from trauma is that children and youth have a strong, caring support system, including you.

❊ ATTENTION DEFICIT DISORDER (ADHD)

ADHD is a chronic condition, meaning this is a long-term diagnosis. You are not here to "cure" the child but to help them (and their parents) learn to cope with it. ADHD can present with or without hyperactivity. Other common problems are difficulty sustaining attention and impulsivity, low self-esteem, poor school performance, and troubled relationships. Some researchers are also beginning to link gut health with ADHD.[3] For some, the symptoms lessen with time, but others continue to struggle into adulthood. Your role is to teach strategies for success.

SYMPTOMS

Inattention
Failing to pay close attention to details
Making careless mistakes
Trouble staying focused on tasks or play
Appearing not to listen, even when spoken to directly
Difficulty following through on instructions
Failing to finish homework or chores
Trouble organizing tasks and activities
Avoiding or disliking tasks that require focused mental effort
Losing items needed for tasks or activities, including toys, pencils, assignments
Easily distracted
Forgetting daily activities, such as brushing teeth or chores
Hyperactivity and impulsivity
Fidgeting, squirming in seat
Difficulty staying seated
"On the go," in constant motion
Running around and climbing in situations where not appropriate
Trouble engaging in quiet play or activity
Talking too much
Blurting out answers, interrupting the question
Difficulty taking turns
Intruding on others' conversations, games, or activities[4]

MOOD DISORDERS

Unlike a normal bad mood common to children, mood disorders are intense, persistent, and difficult to manage. A mood disorder is a medical condition, not something a child will get over.

Common diagnoses in this area include:

Major Depression: A depressed or irritable mood lasting at least two weeks.

Persistent Depressive Disorder (Dysthymia): A chronic, low-grade, depressed, or irritable mood for at least one year.

Bipolar Disorder: Periods of persistently elevated mood followed by periods of depressed or flat emotional response.

Disruptive Mood Dysregulation Disorder: A persistent irritability and extreme inability to control behavior.

Premenstrual Dysphoric Disorder: This includes depressive symptoms, irritability, and tension before menstruation.

Mood disorder due to a medical condition: Many medical illnesses, including cancer, injuries, and chronic medical illnesses, can trigger symptoms of depression.

Substance-induced mood disorder.[5]

BEHAVIORAL DISORDERS

Children who are aggressive, angry, defiant, or argumentative with adults can be diagnosed with a behavioral disorder. Just as in mood disorders, these behaviors go beyond what is normal for children and are intense, persistent, and difficult to manage. Two common behavioral disorders are Oppositional Defiant Disorder (ODD) and Conduct Disorder.

Disruptive, Impulse Control, and Conduct Disorders are problems in self-control of emotions and behaviors. Not every diagnosis that has these issues includes ADHD. These behaviors violate the rights of others or bring the client into significant conflict with authority or societal norms.[6]

EXAMPLES OF ODD BEHAVIOR

Often being angry or losing one's temper
Often arguing with adults
Refusal to comply with adult directives or requests
Deliberately annoying others or being annoyed by others
Blaming others for their own mistakes or misbehaviors

EXAMPLES OF CONDUCT DISORDER

Breaking serious rules, such as running away, staying out at night, or skipping school

Being aggressive in a way that causes harm, such as bullying, fighting, or animal cruelty

Lying, stealing, or damaging property

Positive parenting strategies are important. Family BHIS hours are helpful.[7]

❁ ANXIETY

Anxiety is greater than simple childhood fears and worries. (Do you see a theme here?) An anxiety disorder interferes with school, home, and relationships for children. This may look like anger, irritability, or fear. Be aware that often children can keep this to themselves and a diagnosis may be missed.

Common Anxiety Disorders in Children Include:

Separation Anxiety: Extreme fear when away from parents or caregivers.

Phobia: Extreme fear of a specific thing or situation, such as dogs or going to the doctor.

Social Anxiety: Being afraid of school or other places with people.

General Anxiety: Being worried about the future or about bad things happening.

Panic Disorder: Repeated episodes of sudden, unexpected, intense fear. This comes with physical symptoms such as heart racing, difficulty breathing, etc.[8]

❁ TIC DISORDERS

Tics are repetitive, quick muscle movements that result in sudden, difficult-to-control body jolts or sounds. While tics are common in childhood, they usually decrease over time.

Tics that last more than one year can lead to a diagnosis of Tourette's syndrome. A doctor should be seen if the tics:

Become more frequent or severe
Cause emotional or social problems, including embarrassment, social isolation, or bullying
Cause pain or discomfort, often through non-intentional self-injury
Interfere with school or daily activities
Are accompanied by anger, depression, or self-harm

Symptoms usually begin to appear between the ages of five and ten with simple, mild tics involving the face, head, or arms. In Tourette's syndrome (TS), the frequency, intensity, and number of tics increase and involve more body parts. As they increase, they become more disruptive.

Transient tics are experienced by up to 10 percent of children for between four and twelve months. These tics may be more prevalent during stress, fatigue, or as a side effect of medication and can be confused with nervousness, anxiety, or restlessness in childhood.[9]

AUTISM SPECTRUM DISORDER

Those with Autism Spectrum Disorder (ASD) may behave, communicate, learn, and interact in ways different from neurotypical individuals. They do not look different from anyone else and are not set apart by deficits but by different abilities. They differ greatly in how the deficits they do have appear. Some may be brilliant conversationalists, while others are nonverbal. Some need help in activities of daily living, while others live with little to no outside support.

As children grow, the common areas in which we see difficulty is the ability to develop and maintain relationships, communicate with peers and adults, or understand social norms. Children can come to the attention of healthcare professionals when they experience concurrent anxiety, depression, or ADHD. Attention deficit disorder is more common in people with ASD than in people without ASD.[10]

Summary

Children come to us because of their diagnoses. It is important to know what diagnoses might apply and use those possibilities to shape your work with your client. Remember, you cannot diagnose, but you can ask informed questions of your client, given their age and diagnosis. Use what you understand of their diagnosis or diagnoses to shape how you approach the issue.

Questions for Reflection and Discussion

Your client is an eleven-year-old female with an anxiety diagnosis. When you have a session at school, the teacher wants to talk to you about your client's explosion yesterday. One of her friends made a comment that upset her, and she started yelling and screaming, "I never want to talk to you again!" The other girl's feelings are hurt, and the eight-year-long friendship is suffering. What topics do you discuss in the session?

NOTES

1. David Dubois and Michael Karcher, editors, *Handbook of Youth Mentoring* 2nd Ed., (Sage Publications, 2013).
2. "Child Trauma." SAMHSA, May 2018, https://samhsa.gov/child-trauma/understanding-child-trauma.
3. Trevor Cickovski, et al., "Attention Deficit Hyperactivity Disorder (ADHD) and the gut microbiome: An ecological perspective," *PLoS One*, 2023 Aug 18; 18(8).
4. "Attention-deficit/hyperactivity disorder (ADHD) in Children," Mayo Clinic, Jan. 25, 2023, https://www.mayoclinic.org/diseases-conditions/adhd/symptoms-causes/syc-20350889.
5. "Mood Disorders in Children and Adolescents," Children's Hospital of Philadelphia, March 3, 2023, https://www.chop.edu/conditions-diseases/mood-disorders-children-and-adolescents.
6. Wenzel, Mario & Rowland, Zarah & Bürgler, Sebastian & Hennecke, Marie. (2024). Emotion regulation and self-control: Same same but different... and even incompatible?. Journal of personality, 92. 10.1111/jopy.12965, https://www.researchgate.net/publication/382595052_Emotion_regulation_and_self-control_Same_same_but_different_and_even_incompatible.
7. "Behavior or Conduct Problems in Children," Centers for Disease Control, June 9, 2025, https://www.cdc.gov/children-mental-health/about/about-behavior-or-conduct-problems-in-children.html?CDC_AAref.
8. "Anxiety and Depression in Children, Centers for Disease Control, June 9, 2025, https://www.cdc.gov/children-mental-health/about/about-anxiety-and-depression-in-children.html.
9. Tics and Tourette Syndrome, Boston Children's Hospital, March 13, 2023, https://www.childrenshospital.org/conditions/tourette-syndrome.
10. "About Autism Spectrum Disorder," Centers for Disease Control, April 15, 2025, https://www.cdc.gov/autism/about/index.html; "How to Control Anger in Children." n.d., https://web.archive.org/web/20200712203330/https://www.scholastic.com/parents/family-life/social-emotional-learning/praise-and-discipline/anger-management-children.html.

CHAPTER THREE

ANGER MANAGEMENT AND CONFLICT RESOLUTION

Gilly

Name: Gilly
Age: 12
Gender: Female
Ethnicity: Hispanic
School: Blossom GIRLS Day Program
Health: Poor sleep hygiene
Family Members: Ramona, mom; Joel, eight-year-old brother
Relationship: None
Family Health History: Domestic violence victims; Mom, anxiety; Joel, anxiety
Alcohol/Drug Use: None
Challenges: Single parent, on the run from father, Mom has limited English skills
Goals: Graduate from high school, avoid father, learn anger management skills
Coping Skills: Deep breathing, distractions, cold drinks
Strengths: Compassion, love of family, faith
Weaknesses: No anger management skills, nightmares, single-parent family, abuse victim

Symptoms/Problems: Produced a "kill list," low reading skills possibly due to inattention, no emotional management skills
Diagnosis: CPTSD, ADHD
Treatment Goals/Progress:
Utilize anger management skills to reduce outbursts from five times per week to two times per week
Reduce the frequency of sleep issues by 25 percent in twelve months
Reduce sleep issues intensity by 35 percent in twelve months
Improve focus by 10 percent, as evidenced by improved reading scores within twelve months

Case Conceptualization and Discussion:

❇ ANGER MANAGEMENT

Gilly is a dark-haired beauty who appears happy on the surface but with an unsettling glint in her eyes. She can identify friends among girls in the program but does not display the characteristics of friendships with girls this age. She holds back from them, never opening up.

Five years ago, after her mother found out her father had sexually abused Gilly, she took Gilly and her younger brother on the run. The family lived in fear of his finding them and returning them to a home with violence, abuse, drinking, and drugs.

Gilly has the right to be angry but expresses it in negative ways. She came to therapy after making a "hit list" of fourteen people at school she wanted dead. She had no means to commit homicide, and the reasons she wanted them dead varied from bullying to jealousy.

Anger is not the only emotion Gilly expresses negatively. She tells off-color jokes, appears to enjoy the pain of others, and expresses anger no matter what emotion she feels. Because of the fear her father would find them, Gilly and her family relocate frequently, leaving no trace. Gilly does not have lasting relationships outside of her family. They have been in their current location for nine months, and Mom is talking about moving back to Mexico.

Gilly needs to learn acceptable ways to express anger and correctly identify other emotions. She needs a sense of belonging that comes from having relationships outside of her family that she will not destroy or be pulled away from.

Gilly is working on a program to learn anger management. She resists talking about her abuse, but the core skills still apply, so she is also working on self-esteem and recognizing her strengths. The program has scheduled a doctor's visit to check on the possibility of ADHD.

Gilly's case is perfect to introduce the topics of anger management and conflict resolution. If you could pick one word to describe Gilly, it would be *anger*. A church that could love her in the face of that anger would make a world of difference in her young life.

Know this, my beloved brothers: let every person be quick to hear, slow to speak, slow to anger; for the anger of man does not produce the righteousness of God. (JAMES 1:19–20)

Imagine if Gilly and her family found a church that not only helped teach Gilly anger management but stood as a wall of protection against her father, an angry man.

Anger Management and Conflict Resolution

Anger is a signal emotion. It usually mobilizes a response to danger and is also a form of self-expression and sometimes a child's way of declaring independence. Many things can trigger a child's anger, and sometimes the result is aggression. As children reach kindergarten, anger does not usually explode into aggression because they have learned to hold back such impulsive urges. Over time, as children reach school age, parents can expect more subtle forms of aggression: pouting, sulking, and whining.

It may seem obvious to adults, but young children need to learn that anger is the name they can attach to certain feelings and the physical sensations that come with anger: a pounding heart, heavy breathing, and a feeling of getting warm. You can help your child in the heat of the moment by acknowledging and naming the emotion: "I can see that you are angry right now." Children also need your help in recognizing the triggers that set off these feelings, such as another child grabbing a toy or threatening to hurt them, an adult thwarting their exciting plans or seeming to punish unjustly, or their failing to reach a new goal they have set. Over time, with your help, they will realize that these situations make them want to scream and kick.

Asking children to stifle such powerful feelings will not work. Anger will dribble into unrelated situations, lead to explosions later, or fester until it turns inward. A key to helping your children with managing anger is getting them to question whether aggression gets them what they want.

Five Strategies

It is never too soon to teach your children how to control their anger so that it does not control them. Remember, however, that it is difficult for young children to master these strategies. Your child will need your help—and a lot of practice.

- *Stop.* If your children feel out of control, they should be separated from the person they feel like hurting. They should leave the room.
- *Calm down.* Teach your children to use some calming strategies when they feel the physical symptoms of anger. They can try taking deep breaths, drinking a

glass of water, distracting themselves with a song or a story, or playing alone.

- *Think before you act.* Encourage your children to ask themselves, "What do I want to happen?" Explain that vengeance and retaliation are not worth acting on. Being understood and making things right are worthwhile.
- *Consider the other person's feelings.* Children can begin to show empathy as young as three years old, but they need your help. Try to get them to understand the other person's point of view, just as they want their point of view understood. See if your children can figure out why the other person doesn't understand their side. Could they find another way to get their view across more clearly? Can they try to let it go?
- *Look for possible solutions.* Help your children see beyond "I hate you, and you're no good." See if you can find a compromise that both parties can agree on. Apologizing often helps.

Physical Aggression

Of course, sometimes anger turns into a physical mêlée. Use this as an opportunity to help your child master these aggressive feelings. Here are some things you can do to facilitate anger management for children:

- *Stop the action and restore safety.* It is often necessary to isolate the fighters. Reassure both sides that they will be safe and that they can learn to stay in control and protect themselves.
- *Set limits.* Lay down the law and let children know who is in charge when they are out of control. "No hitting, and if you won't stop it, I will."
- *Follow through with consequences.* Children must face the consequences of their actions if they are to learn

to stop and think before they act. "If you can't be together without hurting each other, then you can't be together. If you want another chance to play, see if you can remember this."

- *Forgive.* Children need to know that their bad behavior has not turned them into bad people. Apologies and making amends help them move from the guilty feelings that come from knowing they were wrong to having hope that they can do better.[1]

Conflict Resolution for Kids

STEP ONE: SELF-CHECK: AM I READY AND WILLING TO SOLVE THE PROBLEM?	**STEP TWO:** HONEST COMMUNICATION (SEE CHAPTER 5)	**STEP THREE:** FIND A SOLUTION
Be calm or wait until you are No arguing or fighting Be honest Listen without interrupting How big is the problem?	Active listening "I" messages It's okay to disagree	What will each person do? The person is not the problem Many possible solutions Plan of action with steps and timeline Adult or peer assistance

Anger management and conflict resolution in kids with mental health issues can be extreme, as we observed in Gilly's case. We use these skills every day in our own lives, whether we recognize it or not. As you role-play with a partner, think about how you handle these issues as an adult and how that needs to change as a child learning how to control their anger.

Activity

Role-Play with a Partner. Choose the role of aggressor in one situation and the victim in the other.

Situation 1: Two children are on the playground. The aggressor wants to swing, and the victim is still on the swing they want.

Situation 2: The child is aggressive about wanting to stay up. The parent is victimized for wanting to adhere to bedtime.

NOTE

1. "How to Control Anger in Children." Scholastic, https://web.archive.org/web/20200712203330/https://www.scholastic.com/parents/family-life/social-emotional-learning/praise-and-discipline/anger-management-children.html.

CHAPTER FOUR

MINDFULNESS AND GROWTH MINDSET

Sally

Name: Sally
Age: 13
Gender: Female
Ethnicity: Asian
School: ABC School
Health: History of congenital Chiari malformation (a condition present at birth where pressure on the brain from a small skull forces the brain stem down into the spinal canal), no current effects; low IQ
Family Members: Molly, mom; Gary, dad; Sue, Mom's best friend; Lou, Dad's aunt; three-year-old brother, Bailey; seventeen-year-old brother, Joey; six-year-old cousin, Becky (Lou); eight-year-old cousin, Tammy (Lou)
Relationship: Tom, seventeen-year-old high school dropout
Family Health History: All adults smoke, seventeen-year-old brother diagnosed with ADHD, also smokes
Alcohol/Drug Use: Unclear
Challenges: IEP (Individualized Education Plan) for reading, math, behaviors; lack of consistent discipline; possible abuse by seventeen-year-old brother
Goals: Listen to adults, quit hitting and screaming, utilize coping skills

Coping Skills: Learned but unused
Strengths: Friendly, loves animals
Weaknesses: Emotional management, learning disabilities
Symptoms/Problems: Lack of compliance with rules, violent outbursts
Diagnosis: ADHD, Specific Learning Disorder with impairment in reading and with impairment in mathematics, ODD (Oppositional Defiant Disorder)
Treatment Goals/Progress:
Comply with list of written rules three times per day from one time per day
Reduce outbursts from seven days per week to four days per week
Develop three positive, age-appropriate relationships by the end of the school year

Case Conceptualization and Discussion:

❃ GROWTH

Sally is a thirteen-year-old girl living in a three-bedroom home with her parents, a three-year-old brother, Mom's best friend, Dad's aunt, two female cousins (ages eight and six), and occasionally her seventeen-year-old brother. The rest of the time, her older brother is in a treatment facility for violence. He once punched a hole in the wall and other times punched his mother, laid hands on Sally, and kicked the family dog. Sally's mother is always at work, trying to provide for such a large family. It is unclear if Dad has a job, but he is gone all day. The two other women are home all day and provide most of the directives.

The household has a lot of rules, but they are vague and interpreted differently by the different women in the house. Sally is expected to obey all directives, even if they are contradictory. Discipline is not followed through, and a lot of yelling is in the home. Sally has an IEP for reading, mathematics, and behavior. She struggles with peer relationships, and most of her friends are older or significantly younger than her. The older ones are not good role models. During the COVID quarantine, when schooling happened at home, Sally's grades improved without the distraction of social situations.

Sally needs the support of a consistent adult. She needs specific, measurable, and realistic rules and consistent enforcement of those rules. She works with her therapist on recognizing the qualities of a good friend and on coping skills for managing frustration. Family BHIS sessions are often canceled and rarely attended by all the adults in the home. Sally could benefit from learning about mindfulness, among other interventions.

Mindfulness is a concept that comes out of Dialectical Behavior Therapy. It refers to being present in the moment and not distracted by worries for the future or regrets from the past. It can be helpful for kids with ADHD to practice being in the moment, apart from distractions that take up much of their lives.

I can do all things through him who strengthens me.
(PHILIPPIANS 4:13)

The church can be an excellent role model of mindfulness and a growth mindset. The Philippians passage summarizes the heart of a growth mindset. Sally can benefit from mindfulness as it teaches her to ignore distractions, and Sally is distracted by everything. It is not her most important need, but mindfulness can affect many areas of need.

Mindfulness and Growth Mindset

The Mayo Clinic tells us that "mindfulness is a type of meditation in which you focus on being intensely aware of what you're sensing and feeling in the moment, without interpretation or judgment. Practicing mindfulness involves breathing methods, guided imagery, and other practices to relax the body and mind and help reduce stress."[1]

Some people like to say they overthink. All too often, children also spend too much time planning, problem-solving, daydreaming, or thinking either random or negative thoughts. Mindfulness directs your attention away from your inner world and into the world around you.[2] It can help to reduce stress, anxiety, and depression. Doctors may even prescribe mindfulness to address pain or high blood pressure.

BREATHING FOR MINDFULNESS

A focus on breathing is an important entry step into mindfulness. Allow your client a choice of proscribed breathing patterns to bring them into this way of thinking. Here are several options for directed breathing:

- *Flower Breath.* Imagine a beautiful, fragrant flower in front of you. Hold it in your hands and notice all the vibrant colors. Breathe slowly and smell the wonderful fragrances. Release the air out of your mouth.
- *Balloon Breath.* Take a deep breath in and exhale through your mouth as if you were blowing up a balloon. Start to spread your hands as if you were holding the balloon. Hold your hands still as you take in a breath through your nose, then expand your hands as you blow up the imaginary balloon. When your balloon is full, raise your hands to the sky as you let your balloon go.
- *Cookie Breath.* Imagine you have your favorite cookie in front of you. Take a big sniff and remember all the tasty smells. The cookie is too hot to eat, so purse your lips and blow on it to cool it. Do this again until it is cool enough to eat.
- *Ocean Waves.* Imagine sitting on the beach. Feel the sand under your hands. As you sit peacefully, imagine

watching the waves gently rise and fall. With each rising wave, breathe in the crisp salt air through your nose. As the wave falls, breathe out through your mouth.

- *Buzzing Bee.* You are a buzzing bee. Spread your arms out like wings. As you breathe in, lift your wings into the air. Hold for a moment. Let your arms fall gently and buzz as you breathe out.
- *Bear Breath.* Imagine you are a sleeping bear hibernating for winter. You are warm, cozy, and safe. Take a deep breath like a sleeping bear. Release that breath as you continue to imagine yourself hibernating in your cozy cave with your cubs.
- *Triangle Breathing.* Draw a triangle in the air with your finger. As you trace the first side, breathe in through your nose. As you trace the second side, hold your breath. Blow out slowly as you trace the third side of the triangle.
- *Heart Breath.* Place your hands over your heart and close your eyes. Think of a happy place and imagine you are there. Feel your chest rise and fall with each breath. Find your peace.

GUIDED MEDITATION AS A MINDFULNESS TOOL

Guided meditation uses paced storytelling with modulated tone and volume to create a peaceful sense of well-being. As you read these stories, decrease your speed and lower your tone and volume as you go.

SCRIPT ONE

When you feel ready, lie back and get comfortable. If you like, you can close your eyes. Let's do some mindful breathing. Take a big breath while you count to three in your head. Hold that breath for a count of three. Now blow out your breath like you would blow out a candle. Blow out on a four count.

In, 2, 3. Hold, 2, 3. Out, 2, 3, 4.

Take two more mindful breaths.

In, 2, 3. Hold, 2, 3. Out, 2, 3, 4.

In, 2, 3. Hold, 2, 3. Out, 2, 3, 4.

It is safe here. My voice will not take you to unsafe places. Let your breathing return to normal as you imagine a special place.

Imagine you are walking in a forest with lots of light streaming through the trees. Up ahead you can see a break in the trees where the light is bright, and a breeze is ruffling the leaves. As you reach the edge of a clearing, you see an area set up for you with a soft blanket and a picnic basket with some snacks and your favorite drink. After you have a snack, you lie back in the shade. You smell wildflowers and feel the breeze on your skin.

Continue to breathe normally as you feel your body soften. Wiggle your toes and allow them to relax. Do the same with your ankles. Imagine a sunbeam caressing your feet. As it travels up your body, you can feel your calves relax, then your thighs.

Feel the warmth of the sunlight reach your stomach and it relaxes, too. Now your chest relaxes, and your arms, your hands, and your shoulders. Imagine the light touching your face and letting your jaw and your forehead relax. The sun also helps you to relax your scalp.

(Pause for a length of time.)

The sun is starting to set, so you sit up slowly and gather your things. Fold the blanket as you breathe normally and pick up your wrappers and bottles. As you slowly come back to the room, take three mindful breaths.

In, 2, 3. Hold, 2, 3. Out, 2, 3, 4.

In, 2, 3. Hold, 2, 3. Out, 2, 3, 4.

In, 2, 3. Hold, 2, 3. Out, 2, 3, 4.

When you are ready, open your eyes and sit up.

SCRIPT TWO (FOR CLOSING AN INCOMPLETE SESSION)

When you feel ready, lie back and get comfortable. If you like, you can close your eyes. Let's do some mindful breathing. Take a big breath while you count to three in your head. Hold that breath for a count of three. Now, blow out your breath like you would blow out a candle. Blow out for a four count.

In, 2, 3. Hold, 2, 3. Out, 2, 3, 4.

Take two more mindful breaths.

In, 2, 3. Hold, 2, 3. Out, 2, 3, 4.

In, 2, 3. Hold, 2, 3. Out, 2, 3, 4.

It is safe here. My voice will not take you to unsafe places. Let your breathing return to normal as you think about your problems.

If they were a shape, what shape would they be? (Allow answer)

What color is that shape? (Allow answer)

Is the shape soft or hard? (Allow answer)

Is it smooth or rough? (Allow answer)

And how big is that shape? (Allow answer)

We want to put that shape away now so we can deal with it later. What kind of container will hold that shape? (Allow answer)

Imagine putting that shape in the container. Is it secure? (Allow answer)

What would make it secure? (Allow answer)

Okay. Do that. Where will you put your container? (Allow answer)

Is it safe there? How can we make it safe? (Allow answer)

Let's do another round of mindful breathing.

In, 2, 3. Hold, 2, 3. Out, 2, 3, 4.

In, 2, 3. Hold, 2, 3. Out, 2, 3, 4.

In, 2, 3. Hold, 2, 3. Out, 2, 3, 4.

When you're ready, sit up slowly and open your eyes. Maybe a gentle stretch, too.[3]

LEAVES ON A STREAM (ADAPTED FROM MULTIPLE SOURCES)

During this exercise, you will visualize yourself resting near a stream. Whenever thoughts enter your mind, imagine placing them on a leaf and casting them on the stream to drift away.

Find a quiet place, free of distractions. Sit or lie down in a comfortable position. Close your eyes or let your gaze grow fuzzy. Begin by taking slow, deep breaths.

Visualize Imagine you are resting beside a stream. The scene can look however you would like. Use all your senses. What do you see? What sounds are there? What does it feel like beside the stream? Notice any sensations that come to mind.

Meditate Focus on the stream. When distractions enter your mind, such as thoughts or feelings, take a moment to notice them without judgment. Treat all your thoughts and feelings the same, whether positive, negative, or neutral. After acknowledging them, bring your thoughts back to the stream. You can imagine writing the distractions on a leaf and dropping it in the water to float away.

Practice Continue visualizing the stream, simply observing and releasing any thoughts that enter your mind. There is nothing else you need to do. You may set a timer for ten to fifteen minutes to let you know when you are finished.[4]

Growth Mindset Questions

A growth mindset is a way of viewing the positive side of events and focusing on developing your abilities. The key phrase is "I can't do that *yet*." Ask these instead of asking how their day went:

What made you feel smart today?
What is one mistake you learned from today?

How will you improve tomorrow?
What do you want to learn?
How do you handle it when you don't understand something?
Who gives you an honest opinion?
What change has made you a better learner?
What goal are you working on?
In what way do you want to grow?
What are you proud of doing today?
When do you like to learn?
What is a positive thing that happened today?
What have you done that you thought was impossible?
What would help you try harder tomorrow?
What does it mean to be a good learner?

Many times, children (especially those in the system for a while) are convinced they have tried everything and are not capable of what we are asking. The growth mindset switches their attitude from what they cannot do to a mindset of *yet*. Encouraging growth makes kids easier to work with by improving their attitude. Often, the biggest barrier for Sally is her attitude. She proved during COVID that she can do the work.

Questions for Reflection and Discussion

Try three or four of the breathing techniques. How do they make you feel? Is there one you would recommend over the others? Talk about the process.

How I Practice Mindfulness Worksheet

In each square, draw or describe four activities that help you stay present and grounded. This may be taking a walk, visiting a museum, or practicing controlled breathing.

NOTES

1. "Mindfulness Exercises." Mayo Clinic. October 11, 2022, https://www.mayoclinic.org/healthy-lifestyle/consumer-health/in-depth/mindfulness-exercises/art-20046356.
2. "Mindfulness Exercises." Mayo Clinic. October 11, 2022, https://www.mayoclinic.org/healthy-lifestyle/consumer-health/in-depth/mindfulness-exercises/art-20046356.
3. Adapted from EMDR Therapy Resourcing Container Exercise, Trauma Therapist Institute, https://www.traumatherapistinstitute.com/blog/Free-EMDR-Container-Exercise-Script-PDF-A-Tool-for-Trauma-Informed-Therapy.
4. Laura K. Schenck, "Leaves on a Stream"—Cognitive Defusion Exercise, Mindfulness Muse, https://www.mindfulnessmuse.com/acceptance-and-commitment-therapy/leaves-on-a-stream-cognitive-defusion-exercise.

CHAPTER FIVE

INTERVENTIONS

Raquel

Name: Raquel
Age: 17
Gender: Trans female
Ethnicity: Hispanic
School: DEF School
Health: Overweight
Family Members: Ramon, father; Susanna, mother; Harold, twelve-year-old brother; Amie, three-year-old sister
Relationship: None
Family Health History: Dad has heart issues, Mom has depression
Alcohol/Drug Use: Underage drinking (cultural), smoking
Challenges: Loss of best friend to suicide, transgender acceptance, mild depression
Goals: To be accepted as female, to improve mood
Coping Skills: Working on cars, listening to music, drinking
Strengths: Working on cars, drawing
Weaknesses: Social acceptance, underage drinking
Symptoms/Problems: Complicated grief, mild depression
Diagnosis: Mild depression
Treatment Goals/Progress:

Develop two healthy coping skills in six months
Strengthen identity as evidenced by improved self-esteem in six months
Complete grieving process within twelve months

Case Conceptualization and Discussion:

GENDER ACCEPTANCE

Raquel is a large person, tall and solid, with a big personality. Born a boy named George, they think of themself as a girl. At school, the guidance counselors are unsure of how to handle this and continue to use their dead name and ignore their pronouns.

Raquel, despite their big personality, is sometimes afraid of how people react to them as a transgender individual. They are uncomfortable using the boys' locker room but also know they are not accepted in the girls' locker room. They sometimes see discrimination when it is not intended, but a lot is intended as well. Raquel's family loves them unconditionally but is unsure of how they should react to "his" problems. In addition, Raquel is grieving for their best friend, who was killed in a car accident that many suspect may have been a suicide.

Raquel needs to be supported in their grief and watched for signs that they might be considering suicide. Their therapist serves as an advocate in the school as well as doing grief work and has found that the grief work sometimes also applies to Raquel's gender transition.

Whatever you do, work heartily, as for the Lord and not for men. (COLOSSIANS 3:23)

Interventions are the heart of the work of the BHIS. And no one works harder for a good cause than church folk. Raquel often finds that interventions closely follow things she has already learned, though in a more formal form. Interventions support the parenting a child receives, but if the parent never learned that skill, their children could instruct them as well.

Interventions

Interventions are activities specifically designed to address a need. They may include games, worksheets, activities, and exercises. The agency I worked for when writing this book had a file with over 250 usable interventions copied from various sources, with another file specifically for telehealth (therapy delivered over a video call). Searches of teacher sites and counseling sites will yield a lot of copyrighted material that you can use for free but cannot be reproduced here.

Some of the tried-and-true techniques are included, such as Stop and Think, Positive Discipline, and I-Statements. Worksheets are a quick go-to, but I caution against what teachers refer to as "drill and kill." Too much of a good thing can turn kids against working with you. Because kids are used to the idea, I like to follow work time (this section) with play time. Activities in the next chapter fit that description. They are fun, and much of the learning is a hidden curriculum.

❃ STOP AND THINK

Stop and Think is an age-appropriate program to teach children impulse control. The key to the program is to first teach the behavior you want displayed. Be sure you are modeling the skill as well. This may be by verbalizing your thought process.

For example: "John is not listening to me. This makes me angry. *Stop and think*: What should I do about it? Make a good choice or make a poor choice? I need him to know I am angry, so I will tell him, but I will stay calm and use I-Statements. What are the steps to a good choice? John, I get angry when you don't listen. I feel disrespected, and I need your attention for me to teach you. Do it!"

Next, role-play the process with kids, walking through it step by step. It is important to give feedback during this process. Now you can prompt the kids to use these skills within the session and outside of the session. Let their teacher know what you are doing so they can do the same thing at school. This same process can be used to teach many social skills.

The steps for using this are:

1. Stop.
2. Do I want to make a good choice or a bad choice?
3. What are the steps I need to take?
4. Take the steps.
5. Good job!

I-STATEMENTS

I-Statements focus on the feelings of the giver rather than on the behavior, thoughts, and characteristics of the receiver. They enable the speaker to avoid accusations while still being assertive.

The I-Statement formula is I feel __________ because ________________. When ____________________, I need ________________.

Stating Your Feeling: State your real feeling only, and it starts with the word "I." I feel ______. Focus on the feeling rather than assigning blame. You-Statements ("You make me so mad") usually make the other person defensive. Avoiding these lays the groundwork for positive results.

Connecting the Feeling to an Issue: What issue or event does this concern? ("I feel angry when _______") Now the focus is on the speaker's uncomfortable feeling.

Stating What You Want to Have Happen: Offer a solution ("I would like ______"). Even if this solution is not possible or will be ineffective, it opens the discussion for the other person to become part of the solution rather than the problem.

❁ POSITIVE DISCIPLINE

Based on work by Jane Nelson, Positive Discipline is a system used by schools and parents that emphasizes a focus on the positive over the negative. Not to be confused with behaviorism, true positive discipline is based on five principles. There are no bad children, just bad behaviors. Look for schools to refer to PBIS or positive behavior intervention. Benefits for the child include:

Belonging and Significance: Children feel a sense of connection to the authority
Respectful and Encouraging: Equally kind and firm
Long-Term Results
Teaches Social Skills and Life Skills
Power and Autonomy: Children discover that they are capable

Rules are created to be clear and fair. When not done in advance, this may lead to arbitrary rules with inconsistent application and inconsistent consequences, leading to the failure of discipline. Positive discipline looks to create intrinsic motivation instead of having children follow rules in the hope of reward or fear of punishment. In Positive Discipline, misbehavior is seen as communication that the child has a need not being met, reflecting upon Maslow's Hierarchy of Needs.[1] It also looks toward redirecting behavior rather than becoming a constant no.[2]

Positive discipline is based on mutual respect between the kids and the adults. The adult models firmness in respecting both themselves and the needs of the situation. They model kindness by respecting the child and their needs. To do this they must identify what the child believes that is leading to the behavior. By focusing on solutions rather than on punishment, adults can create discipline that teaches without being punitive. Effective communication skills make this more effective, as does encouragement that notices effort made and improvements rather than success.[3]

Pillars of Character

You may have heard of five, six, or twelve pillars of character. Many schools have adopted the idea of six pillars of character in their SEL (Social and Emotional Learning) curricula. The Six Pillars of Character comprise six ethical characteristics and values, including:

PILLAR ONE: TRUSTWORTHINESS

Teaching your children about trustworthiness means teaching them to do the right thing, being reliable and loyal and standing by his or her family. Kids should also be taught not to deceive, cheat, or steal under the trustworthiness pillar. Round up your kids and give each one a balloon. Have them blow up their balloon and tell them that the balloon they are holding signifies a lie. Rope off an area of your yard or home and instruct your kids to stay within the boundary. But there's a catch. The kids have to toss up their balloons and keep their balloons in the air without leaving the boundary. When the balloon touches the ground, the lie is discovered.

PILLAR TWO: RESPECT

Respect should be taught early in life. One way to teach respect is to take your child outdoors and take a tour of your local walking or hiking trails or a park. Explore the sights, sounds, flowers, dirt, and rocks, explaining that all living creatures should get respect. That means treating people and living things the way you would like to be treated. If you find that your child enjoys stomping on flowers and squishing bugs for fun, it may be time to have a talk about respect.

❁ PILLAR THREE: RESPONSIBILITY

It is never too early to teach your kids about responsibility. Think toddler age. Have your kids help you around the house with chores, enlist their help to make dinner, or give them some responsibility for the family pet. Older elementary-age kids and preteens can also learn responsibility by learning about the outdoors and using airsoft guns. Use this time and activity to teach your kids what it means to be a responsible gun owner, to never point their weapon at another person, and to explain what it is not used for. This is also a great way to share your love of the outdoors and outdoor sporting activities with your kids.

❁ PILLAR FOUR: FAIRNESS

Parents can use role-playing to teach their children about fairness. Consider a puppet show and dialogue that focuses on making a fair decision. Teach your child about the diplomatic way to resolve a situation.

❁ PILLAR FIVE: CARING

Teaching your child to be kind, compassionate, and considerate of others should also start at a young age. Teach children to put themselves in someone else's shoes. Consider putting together sack lunches for those less fortunate in your community with a group or organize a sock drive with other community members. When your child grows up, you can know that they will always help others in need because of your lessons.

❁ PILLAR SIX: CITIZENSHIP

Getting involved with the school or community is a great way to teach citizenship. For example, you can organize or join a group to plant trees in parks around the local community. You and your child can also become a member of an organization that helps clean up the community by removing trash and graffiti. Ample opportunities are out there to help teach citizenship. Which will you choose?[4]

You can engage kids in drawing what they think an emotional face looks like.

Movement

High-intensity interval training (HIIT) has been shown to help in the work of emotional regulation. In just a few minutes with short, intense bursts of energy, kids can begin to manage their emotions and cope with difficult situations. This can be especially important for kids who are neurodiverse, having autism, ADHD, or Sensory Processing Disorder. The stress hormone cortisol is responsible for this relief. When we are dysregulated, our brains produce high levels of cortisol and adrenaline. These chemicals, in turn, increase dysregulation, leading to lowered social communication and executive functioning. Some researchers believe IQ can drop by sixty points during this time.

Exercise reduces these chemicals and increases the production of dopamine, a chemical that can improve synaptic function. Try forty-five-second intervals with fifteen seconds of rest, totaling seven minutes.

Kids find it more enticing when you liken the movements to animals. Hop back and forth like a frog. Walk on hands and feet with hips held high like a bear. Get into a sumo squat with hands on the floor and shuffle like a gorilla. Run as fast as you can like a cheetah. Do jumping jacks with your hands and legs spread wide like a starfish. Sit, place your palms on the floor behind you near your hips, and crawl like a crab. March in place while lifting your knees high and do an elephant stomp.[5]

Feelings

Feelings can be a pressure cooker. If they are not expressed, they can blow up. Expressing feelings can be difficult for people, especially little people who do not yet have the words for what they feel. The following list can be helpful, ranging from simple words that a child understands to more complex. This list can be used to find a more specific word. If someone says they are bored, do they mean indifferent, or do they mean apathetic? Conversely, if they say overwhelmed, do they mean stressed or anxious?

Angry	Let Down	Betrayed
		Resentful
	Humiliated	Disrespected
		Ridiculed
	Bitter	Indignant
		Violated
	Mad	Furious
		Jealous
	Aggressive	Provoked
		Hostile
	Frustrated	Infuriated
		Annoyed
	Distant	Withdrawn
		Numb
	Critical	Skeptical
		Dismissive

Happy	Playful	Aroused
		Cheeky
	Content	Joyful
		Free
	Interested	Curious
		Inquisitive
	Proud	Successful
		Confident
	Accepted	Respected
		Valued
	Powerful	Courageous
		Creative
	Peaceful	Loving
		Thankful
	Trusting	Sensitive
		Intimate
	Optimistic	Hopeful
		Inspired

Surprised	Startled	Shocked
		Dismayed
	Confused	Disillusioned
		Perplexed
	Amazed	Astonished
		Awe
	Excited	Eager
		Energetic

Sad	Hurt	Embarrassed
		Disappointed
	Depressed	Inferior
		Empty
	Guilty	Remorseful
		Ashamed
	Lonely	Isolated
		Abandoned
	Vulnerable	Victimized
		Fragile
	Despair	Grief
		Powerless

Fearful	Scared	Helpless
		Frightened
	Anxious	Overwhelmed
		Worried
	Insecure	Inadequate
		Inferior
	Weak	Worthless
		Insignificant
	Rejected	Excluded
		Persecuted
	Threatened	Nervous
		Exposed

Disgusted	Disapproving	Judgmental
		Embarrassed
	Disappointed	Appalled
		Revolted
	Awful	Nauseated
		Detestable
	Repelled	Horrified
		Hesitant

Bad	Bored	Indifferent
		Apathetic
	Busy	Pressured
		Rushed
	Stressed	Overwhelmed
		Out of Control
	Tired	Sleepy
		Unfocused

Seven Cs of Resilience

This is a list proposed by Kenneth Ginsburg of characteristics that build resilience in kids and adults.

Competence: The ability to handle challenges effectively
Confidence: Belief in your abilities
Connection: Strong, supportive relationships
Character: Strong sense of right and wrong
Contribution: Understanding of the importance of personal contribution to society
Coping: Skills and strategies to manage challenges
Control: Knowing what you influence in your life and environment

Draw where kids experience different emotions in their body.

Additional Breathing Techniques

TRIANGLE BREATHING: Breathe in through the nose for a count of three. Hold for a count of three. Blow out through pursed lips (like blowing bubbles) for a count of three.

FOUR-SEVEN-EIGHT BREATHING (ADVANCED): Breathe in through the nose for a count of four. Hold for a count of seven. Blow out through pursed lips (like blowing bubbles) for a count of eight.

TRACED BREATHING: Trace a shape while following an in/hold/out/hold pattern.

DIAPHRAGMATIC BREATHING: While this technique can be practiced while standing or sitting, lying down helps most people do it correctly. Place one hand on your chest and one hand on your belly. Breathe in through your nose for about two seconds, feeling your stomach expand. The hand on your chest should barely move at all. Purse your lips (as if you are about to drink through a straw), press gently on your stomach, and exhale slowly for about two seconds. Again, the hand on your chest should barely move. Repeat.

ALTERNATE NOSTRIL BREATHING (ADVANCED): Exhale completely and then use your right thumb to close your right nostril. Inhale through your left nostril and then close the left nostril with your fingers. Open the right nostril and exhale through this side. Inhale through the right nostril and then close this nostril. Open the left nostril and exhale through the left side. This is one cycle. Repeat.

Radical Acceptance

When clients come up against something they cannot change, it may benefit them to accept that thing. This is one of the tenets of Dialectical Behavior Therapy.

Possible responses to a problem

Solve the problem
Change your reaction
Radical acceptance
Stay miserable

Steps to Radical Acceptance

Focus on one set of problems at a time
The past is past and cannot be changed
The present also cannot change
The future has limitations

While radical acceptance is an action taken by the client, active listening benefits everyone when everyone does it. Active listening involves preparing to listen, observing verbal and nonverbal communication, and providing appropriate feedback. It is listening to understand rather than listening to respond. The goal is a clear understanding as well as preventing misunderstanding.

Active Listening

Steps to Active Listening:

Be attentive
Summarize
Ask open-ended questions
Request clarification
Show empathy

Use open body language

OR

B: Body language
U: Understanding
I: Interrupting never
L: Look them in the eye
D: Don't judge[6]

Safety Plan

Occasionally, a BHISP may encounter a client showing signs of being suicidal. If this happens and it is safe to do so, tell the parents. If the parents are not safe, you need to have already developed a safety plan within your program. This may include the emergency room or a call to the client's primary care provider (PCP). You can create a safety plan with your client to outline how they can keep themselves safe.

Suicide is not bound by age, race, intelligence, or any other distinctive category. We do not like to think about it, but second graders are not immune to suicidal thoughts. Neither is anyone. Talking about suicide does not increase the risk of it happening. Just the opposite. If someone talks about suicide, pay attention. It is not just for attention. People who attempt or complete suicide are not cowardly or weak. There are almost always warning signs before a suicidal act.[7]

Assess the situation using the MALS acronym. Has the client identified a *method*? Is that method *accessible*? Is it *lethal?* How *specific* are the plans? The more positive responses, the more serious the threat.

When using MALS, remember it is a tool. Your intuition is also important. In the opening case study, there was concern that Raquel might become suicidal. Having a friend who completed suicide raises one's susceptibility. When assessing Raquel's risk, the therapist looked at the method. The friend used a car accident, so it was in Raquel's mind. If we consider accessibility: They owned three cars and had access to others. Lethality: This method has a comparatively low lethality.[8] Specific: Raquel's plans were non-specific: "Someday it might happen." While Raquel's ideation should be addressed, it is not a high-risk situation.

Workbook:

Practice the four breathing techniques in this chapter. Describe the physical sensations you experienced while engaging in them.

____

____

____

____

____

____

____

____

____

____

NOTES

1. Saul McLeod, Maslow's Hierarchy of Needs, *SimplyPsychology*, Updated March 2025, www.simplypsychology.org/maslow.html.
2. *Positive Discipline*, www.positivediscipline.com/about-positive-discipline.
3. Jane Nelson, "Five Criteria for Positive Discipline," *Positive Discipline*, www.positivediscipline.com/about-positive-discipline.
4. Lauren Topor, "Instill the 6 Pillars of Character with These Activities," *IdentityMagazine*, www.identitymagazine.net/2016/08/25/instill-the-6-pillars-of-character-with-these-activities/.
5. "7 Minute HIIT Workout for Kids." Raising an Extraordinary Person. 2025, https://learn.hes-extraordinary.com/7-minute-hiit-workout-for-kids.
6. Jacob Morgan, "5 Ways to Practice Active Listening," *Medium*, July 28, 2021, https://jacobm.medium.com/5-ways-to-practice-active-listening-924b58746494.
7. Pravesh Sharma, "8 Common Myths about Suicide." Mayo Clinic Health System. October 11, 2024, https://www.mayoclinichealthsystem.org/hometown-health/speaking-of-health/8-common-myths-about-suicide.
8. Ziyi Cai, et al., "The lethality of suicide methods: A systematic review and meta-analysis," *Journal of Affective Disorders*, Volume 300, 2022: 121–129, ISSN 0165-0327, https://doi.org/10.1016/j.jad.2021.12.054.

CHAPTER SIX

ACTIVITIES

Manuel

Name: Manuel
Age: 10
Gender: Male
Ethnicity: Hispanic
School: ABC School
Health: Good health
Family Members: Ana, grandmother; Joe, grandma's paramour; Arturo, six-year-old brother; Hannah, three-year-old sister; José, father
Relationship: None
Family Health History: None noted
Alcohol/Drug Use: None
Challenges: Cultural differences between Grandma and client, complicated grief, English language learner (ELL)
Goals: Be a good boy, complete the grieving process
Coping Skills: Drawing, breathwork
Strengths: Drawing, friendly, hard worker, well-liked
Weaknesses: Limited English proficiency
Symptoms/Problems: Overwhelmed by grief, needs advanced coping skills, cultural conflict
Diagnosis: Depression

Treatment Goals/Progress:

Complete the grieving process within the next twelve months

Develop a better relationship with Grandma in the next six months

Improve coping skills as evidenced by independent use of two skills within three months

Improve self-esteem, as evidenced by making three statements of strengths within three months

Case Conceptualization and Discussion:

POST-TRAUMATIC STRESS

Manuel is a ten-year-old male. He and his siblings, a six-year-old brother and a three-year-old sister, live with his maternal grandmother and her boyfriend. Grandma did not want to take them in, but their father, whom she does not like or trust, was not good to care for them. Her daughter had already left the children's father when Manuel found his mother's dead body in their home last summer. The family does not discuss the cause of death, but foul play is not suspected.

Manuel is a thoroughly American boy, but his grandma raised her children according to another culture, and she and Manuel do not understand each other. Grandma is clear in who is her favorite, Manuel's little sister. At school, Manuel is a model student. He has no behavioral issues aside from having days when he is sad. Grandma refers to him and his little brother as "devils" and says they are bad. He has nightmares that he cannot recount, so Grandma thinks he is making it up. She also states she had it worse and thinks he should never play video games. His father visits on the weekends, but Manuel does not look forward to it. He thinks Dad favors his little brother.

Manuel needs help understanding his cultural differences and navigating how he relates to each culture. He needs to be cared for without reservation, and he needs to have his self-worth reinforced. His therapist works with him on his self-worth, incorporating his desire to be in the military and his artistic abilities.

But someone will say, "You have faith and I have works." Show me your faith apart from your works, and I will show you my faith by my works.
(JAMES 2:18)

To be honest, this is my favorite chapter. So many of the activities I use were learned in Vacation Bible School or Girl Scouts and needed to be tweaked to serve mental health needs. The church is a great idea for providing these same services to kids in need because they already know how to teach through activities. Buckle up—this is where the fun stuff is.

Using Activities

JUSTIFICATION

The important thing to note about activities is the justification for their use. What distinguishes a BHIS counselor from a mentor is the reasoning behind why we do these activities. For each activity, many justifications can be found, so I do not have each activity marked with a tag. For example, the friendship bracelet activity can be used as part of a discussion of the qualities of positive friendship, to discuss patterns and habituation, and as a calming technique by thinking of good friends while weaving.

New activities are easy to find. Search scouting websites, teaching websites, and Pinterest activities for kids. Most of these activities are based on activities from those sources. Behavioral interventions can be as diverse as your imagination. Modify your choices. For example, a pumpkin matching game can be turned into apples, and we can add the names of emotions to match with physical signs of that feeling.

❋ THERAPY ACTIVITIES, RECIPES, AND DIRECTIONS

*Recipes marked with an asterisk are ones I have personally tested with clients.

STRESS BALLS

*Use high-quality balloons, two per ball.
Place one tablespoon of water beads into a bowl of water.
The beads will take two to three hours to expand fully.
Have one person hold open the neck of a balloon while the second person scoops in the expanded water beads.
Tie securely at the neck, trim off excess neck with scissors.
Place the first balloon inside the second balloon and again tie and trim the neck.

KINETIC SAND

*Mix ½ cup sand (I use colored sand) with 1 cup flour.
In a separate container, mix ¼ cup vegetable oil with 1 Tbsp water. If using white sand, add food coloring to this mixture.
Add dry mixture to wet, not the other way, or it will clump.
Mix thoroughly. If necessary, add more oil, ¼ tsp at a time.

GROWING CRYSTALS

In a beaker, stir 1/2 cup of Epsom salt with 1/2 cup of very hot tap water for at least one minute.
Add a couple of drops of food coloring if you want your crystals to be colored.
Put the beaker in the refrigerator.
Check on it in a few hours to see a beaker full of crystals.

PLAY DOUGH (SOFT)

*One part hair conditioner is added to two parts of cornstarch.
Food coloring may be added to the conditioner.
Note: This is *messy*.

THERAPY PUTTY (FIRM)

Add 1 cup cornstarch to bowl.

Squeeze 3 to 4 oz. of hand lotion into your bowl of cornstarch.

Mix it with your spoon and then your hands, knead the dough until smooth.

Optional: Add 1 to 2 drops of color to the lotion and mix.

Optional: Add 1 drop of essential oils to the complete putty.

Note: This, too, is *messy*.

BUBBLES

Whisk ½ cup sugar and 4 cups warm water until the sugar dissolves.

Whisk in ½ cup blue Dawn dish soap.

Letting the homemade bubbles sit for a couple of hours, or even overnight, helps them work better, but it is not necessary.

OOBLEK

*Mix one part water with two parts cornstarch.

ICE CREAM IN A BAG

½ cup half and half

1 Tbsp. sugar

¼ tsp. vanilla

Put all ingredients in a zip-seal sandwich bag. Make sure the seal is tight.

In a gallon-sized zip-seal bag, place the smaller bag, and add:

3 cups crushed ice

1/3 cup rock salt

Squeeze the larger bag to mix the smaller bag. It should be complete in 10 to 15 minutes. This gets *very* cold, so you may want to hold your contraption in a towel or wear gloves.

❃ SENSORY BOTTLES

RAIN STICK: Choose an empty water bottle. I like Voss, but the lid will break if used roughly. Peel off the sticker on the bottle and remove any sticky residue with Goo Gone. Fill the recycled bottle with small sticks and twigs. Tangle them up and in different directions rather than sticking them all straight into the bottle. This will create more surface area for the rice to bounce off to produce the sound of rain. Add 5 to 10 teaspoons of rice to the rain stick musical sensory bottle. Put the lid on your bottle and play with it to see if you like the sound it makes. You can adjust the amount of rice to change the sound. This could also be done with small pebbles.

GLITTER BOTTLE: *Choose a bottle that can withstand hot water. If needed, take off the label and use Goo Gone to remove any sticky residue. Pour 1 1/2 cups of boiling hot water into a 1-quart measuring cup.

Boiling water is the best for making sensory bottles with glitter glue because it helps the glue, water, and glitter mix well. It may melt the bottle, though, so test first. I've melted a few.

Squeeze 1/3 bottle (2 oz) of blue glitter glue or 2 oz of clear glue into the hot water and mix well with a whisk. Add pinches and shakes of hexagon glitter, flake glitter, and fine glitter in the color combination of choice. Mix well with a wire whisk while the water is still boiling hot. Pour the mixture into your chosen bottle. You may need to use your fingers to get some of the glitter into your bottle, but do not worry about every flake. Add a drop or two of liquid watercolors (not too much, as a tiny drop goes a *long* way) to give your glitter sensory bottle a primary color. Place the lid on the bottle and give it a shake. Need more glitter or liquid watercolor? Add it in before topping it off with water. Use super glue or another strong adhesive to attach the lid.

GLOW IN THE DARK: Prepare the water bottle. Fill the bottle halfway with water. Drop glow-in-the-dark loom bands or other glow-in-the-dark items into the bottle. Add a few drops of glycerin. This is what snow globes use. It makes the loom bands swirl better than with water alone. Fill the bottle the rest of the way with water. You want to fill it all the way to the top so there is no air in it. Place the lid on the bottle and shake it up.

WATER BEADS: Prepare the bottle. Set the water beads to grow in a different container. Only add them to your sensory bottle after they have reached full size (several hours). Place them in the sensory bottle and add water to the top. Glue the lid in place.

LAVA BOTTLE: Fill the bottle ¾ of the way with water. Add in food coloring, but do not go too dark. Add vegetable oil, leaving about a half-inch space at the top. Next, add a teaspoon of table salt before capping the bottle.

**FRIENDSHIP BRACELETS ON A LOOM:*

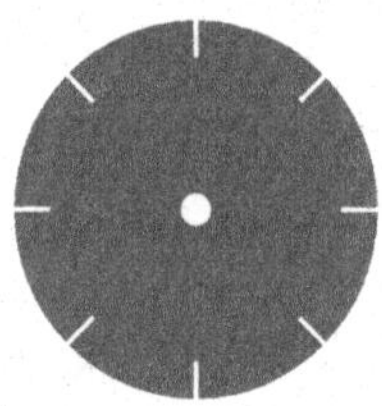

Pattern for loom: Make from cardboard or heavy foam. The circle may be any size with a hole in the middle and 8 slots along the edge. Use yarn or embroidery floss.

Take 7 strands of yarn (3 ft) and tie a knot at one end.

Thread your strands through the hole in the disc.

Take one strand at a time and slot it through one of the slots.

Take the third strand to the *left* of the spare slot, lift it, bring it down, and put it through the empty slot. This creates a new empty space.

Rotate your disc for the empty slot to point and again, pick the strand third to the left and bring down. Repeat.

Your yarn friendship bracelet will begin to "grow" on the other side of the disc, giving it a gentle tug every so often.
For a good video of this, visit RedTedArt at https://www.redtedart.com/friendship-bracelets-with-cardboard/.

Therapy Games for Kids with Movement

RED LIGHT, GREEN LIGHT: Kids move on the green light and stop on the red light. Do not get caught moving on the red light.

MOTHER MAY I: One child is the leader. The rest of the children ask, "Mother, may I take. . . ." a certain number of steps, hops, jumps, or leaps to get to the leader. The leader approves or disapproves.

FREEZE DANCE: Turn on music. When music stops, children must freeze.

FOLLOW MY CLAP: The leader creates a clapping pattern. Children must listen and repeat.

LOUD OR QUIET: Children must perform an action either loudly or quietly. First, pick an action like stomping feet. The leader says, "Loud," and the children stomp their feet loudly. The same directions for "quiet."

SIMON SAYS: Children have to perform an action only when the leader says, "Simon says. . . ." For example, if the leader says, "Simon says touch your toes," and all the children touch their toes. If the leader says, "Touch your toes," nobody should touch their toes.

BODY PART MIX-UP: The leader will call out body parts for the children to touch. For example, the leader calls out "knees," and the children touch their knees. Create one rule to start. Each time the leader says "head," touch your toes instead of your head. This requires the children to stop and think about their actions and not just react. The leader calls out "knees, head, elbow." The children should touch their knees, toes, and elbows. Continue practicing and adding other rules to change body parts.

FOLLOW THE LEADER: The leader performs different actions, and the children must follow the actions exactly.

READY, SET, WIGGLE: The leader calls out, "Ready...Set... Wiggle," and everyone wiggles their bodies. The leader calls out, "Ready...Set...Watermelon," and no one should move. The leader calls out. "Ready...Set...Wigs," and no one moves. The leader calls out, "Ready...Set...Wiggle," and everyone wiggles again. You can change this to whatever wording you want. The purpose is to have the children wait to move until a certain word is said out loud.

COLOR MOVES: Explain to children that they will walk around the room. They are to move based on the color of the paper that you are holding up. Green paper means walking fast, yellow paper means going at a regular pace, and blue paper means walking slowly. Whenever you hold up a red paper, they stop. Try different locomotor skills, like running in place, marching, or jumping.

Therapy Activities (Tweens/Teens)

ALTER THE IMAGE: For the art project, your teen will love the creativity that comes along. The best part about this activity is that your teens do not have to be artistically inclined or good at art. All they need with them is magazine cutouts of people's portraits and faces.

Let the teens deface the images, but in a way that makes them look beautiful, artistic, and nice, but not ruined. The idea is to help your teens learn the difference between perception and respecting others' feelings. Try to get the images in large sizes so that the teens have a bigger surface area to work on. Let them use an assortment of oil pastels and other art materials that they love.

WORDS I WILL LIVE BY: In trying to create a collage of positive and inspirational words, the teens can express motivational thoughts and ideas. You can let each teen create a personal collage of different inspirational quotes/words or let them create one big project that involves the sharing of thoughts and ideas. Hand out craft paper to the teens or use a big poster paper for creating the collage. Then ask the teens to write out their thoughts and positive words on paper, using various designs and art supplies. Alternatively, they can cut out words or letters from magazines to make their poster. Once it is done, let each teen keep it on his or her desk as a positive daily reminder.

CONNECT WITH THE LYRICS: You can choose some songs that you want to use for the activity in advance. Let all the teens sit down and then play the song. Once it is over, ask them to write down the meaning of the song in their own words and how they connect with and interpret it. The teens can do a small rendition of the lyrics to write a paragraph or more about what it made them think of and what it made them feel like. Once the teens are comfortable opening up like this, you can also ask them to get more creative and come up with similar lyrics.

CREATING HEADLINES: Hand out the front page of a newspaper to each teen or ask them to bring one from home. Next, hand them a piece of blank paper and a pen and let them glue it on the newspaper in such a way that it looks as if the blank space is to be filled out with a news item. The teens will have to write a headline that will describe them best. Leave the ideas free so that it could be anything about their personality—something they are good at or they feel strongly about. Let them come up with interesting topics. Once the headline part is over, ask them to write out a full paragraph or more to elaborate on the headline. It is a great activity that will let the teens express themselves better, as well as understand themselves from a better perspective.

Single-Player Games to Purchase

RORY STORY CUBES

Pros: Can be used as a multiplayer game or as a single-player game. It jump-starts imagination and is great for creative storytelling.

Cons: The icons are sometimes confusing as to what they mean. There is no explanation in the instructions that come with the game.

RUSH HOUR (AVAILABLE AS PHYSICAL OR TABLET VERSIONS)

Pros: Engaging and requires a lot of logical thinking and spatial reasoning. Does not require reading.

Cons: Higher-level challenges can be frustrating.

MIGHTY MIND

Pros: Does not require reading and is appropriate for younger kids. Colorful and can be packed in a relatively small box. Children can build from suggestions or experiment with their designs.

Cons: Pieces can get easily lost. Does not scale well with age.

Pen and Pencil Games and Activities

ZENTANGLES: Doodling is done out of boredom (most notably on the margins in one's class notes) and mindlessness (the doodles are not related to what you are doing at the time), while Zentangle is focused on creating pattern designs and mindfulness (you are purposely drawing something).

TESSELLATIONS: A pattern of shapes that fit perfectly together. A tessellation (or tiling) covers a surface with a pattern of flat shapes so there are no overlaps or gaps.

DOTS AND BOXES: The game starts with an empty grid of dots. Usually, two players take turns adding a single horizontal or vertical line between two unjoined adjacent dots. A player who completes the fourth side of a 1×1 box earns one point and takes another turn.

CATEGORIES: In this game, you will be presented with different categories and asked to come up with a word that begins with a certain letter in each category.

HANGMAN: Hangman is a paper-and-pencil guessing game for two or more players. One player thinks of a word, phrase, or sentence, and the other tries to guess it by suggesting letters within a certain number of guesses.

TIC-TAC-TOE: a paper-and-pencil game for two players, X and O, who take turns marking the spaces in a 3×3 grid. The player who succeeds in placing three of their marks in a horizontal, vertical, or diagonal row is the winner.

PICTIONARY: Players secretly write down common phrases on pieces of paper and fold them up. The first chosen artist randomly picks a phrase, then must draw and get the others to guess the phrase without talking or drawing letters or symbols. Once guessed correctly, a new artist is picked. Variation: Instead of common phrases, write books, characters/celebrities, or films.

PICTURE DICTATION: Players secretly draw a simple object on pieces of paper and fold them up. One person picks a slip of paper and describes the lines without naming the object, while the others draw what has been described. Let everyone take a turn describing.

PAPER TELEPHONE: Three or more people each begin with a piece of paper. At the top of the page, they all draw a picture and pass the paper to the next player. With this new piece of paper, each person writes a caption sentence below the picture, then folds the top of the paper over so only the sentence can be seen. This piece of paper is then passed to the next player, who will draw a picture to go along with the sentence. Each player again folds the paper, now so only the picture can be seen, and passes it along. The game continues until there is no more room, and every player can open the paper and be amused.

CONSEQUENCES: Each player folds their sheet of paper in thirds. They draw a head with the neck toward the fold. Fold the paper so the head is inside, then pass the paper. When the next player gets the paper, they draw the body without looking at the head. Turn the paper drawing side down and pass the paper to the next person. Without looking at what came before, draw the legs. The point of the game is the fun of seeing the resulting pictures.

BATTLESHIP: Each player draws two 10 x 10 grids labeled along the sides with letters and numbers. On the left-hand grid, the player secretly draws rectangles representing their fleet of ships (2 blocks, 3 blocks (2), 4 blocks, 5 blocks). Check out http://www.papg.com/.

I AM: Ask your teen to collect various design objects, such as scrapbook paper, stickers, colorful pens, paper cutouts, graphic design cutouts, self-made printables, real trinkets that your teen uses or has collected, and anything that is like an extension of your teen's personality.

MY HAPPIEST MEMORY: For this activity, your teen will have to recreate a memory that he or she feels is one of their happiest. Ask the teen to act out the memory and describe what was so good about it.

IDENTIFY: Hand out a paper and pen to each teen, along with art pens. The teens must write out their initials on paper and then use it to make any art they want. This is a simple exercise in which the teens can create art as simple or as elaborate as they want.

IMAGINATION: What can you see when you put on your magic glasses? Draw and decorate glasses and finish the picture.

TANGRAM: A paper pattern that can be cut out and arranged into many different shapes. Glue to light cardboard (cereal box) for more durability.

Try to make these items from your tangram blocks: boat, dog, cat, man with a hat, house.

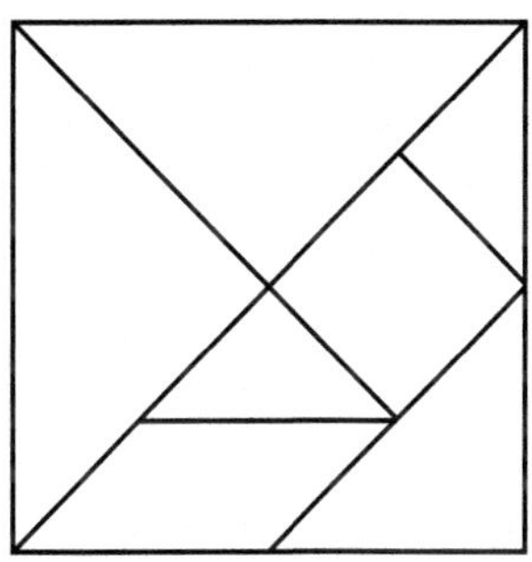

Any Game Questions

Use these questions with any game by answering questions based on the color landed on, the number rolled, or the number spun. Use questions that address the client's current focus. Come up with questions for other topics. Add the questions to the blocks of a Jenga tower. You can even make up a game or have your clients make up one based on their lives. Decorate the board and get your game on.

❇ BREATHING PRACTICE

1. Draw a sideways 8 with your finger. Breathe in on the right half and breathe out on the left half. Pause in the middle.
2. Lay on your back with a stuffed animal on your stomach. Watch the stuffie rise and fall as you breathe.
3. Trace your hand. Inhale as you trace up the fingers. Exhale as you trace down the fingers.
4. Breathe out like you're filling up a balloon. Keep your lungs empty as you imagine the balloon floating away.
5. Breathe in through your nose. Breathe out like you're blowing out a candle.
6. Breathe in like you're smelling a cookie fresh from the oven. It's hot. Blow it off.

❇ GRATITUDE

1. Name a person for whom you are grateful.
2. Name something in nature for which you are grateful.
3. Name a place for which you are grateful.
4. Name something at home for which you are grateful.
5. Name a memory for which you are grateful.
6. Name something or someone at school for whom you are grateful.

❇ GROWTH MINDSET

1. What is something you can do that you couldn't do before?
2. Name a reason mistakes are good.
3. What is one thing you wish you knew?

4. Think of something you are not good at. Say, "I'm not great at [this thing] *yet.*"
5. Name something you did that was hard but fun.
6. What can you tell yourself when the teacher gives you a hard assignment?

ATTENDANCE

1. What is one thing you can do in the morning to be ready on time?
2. How do you feel about school?
3. What is one thing you can do at night to be ready for school?
4. What can happen if you miss too much school?
5. Name one thing you like about school.
6. What is one thing that can happen if you come on time to school every day?

COPING SKILLS

1. Practice a breathing technique and explain what it is.
2. Think about a place that makes you happy. What do you see, hear, feel, taste, and smell?
3. Make all your muscles tight for three seconds. Then, relax them for three seconds.
4. Tell a joke.
5. Tell how you feel and say, "And that's okay."
6. What is one way to express your feelings and get them out of your brain?

SOCIAL SKILLS

1. How do you show someone that you are listening?
2. Practice giving someone a compliment.
3. Name something kind you can do for someone.
4. Practice asking someone a question about themselves.
5. How big is your bubble right now?
6. Name a situation when your thoughts shouldn't be said aloud.

❋ SELF-ESTEEM

1. Name something you are good at.
2. Name a way you can be helpful.
3. Name a goal you have.
4. Give a positive word to describe yourself.
5. Complete the sentence: "I am amazing because . . ."
6. Say, "I am awesome!" three times.

❋ GETTING TO KNOW YOU

1. What is one thing you really like?
2. Name a goal, hope, or dream you have.
3. What is one thing you don't like?
4. Describe one family member.
5. Tell me about one favorite thing.
6. Name one thing in your life you wish was different.

❋ CHOICES AND CONSEQUENCES

1. Describe a choice you made that had good consequences.
2. Describe a choice you made that had bad consequences.
3. Think about a time you got in trouble. What could you have done differently?
4. Describe a choice you get to make at school.
5. Name a choice that adults make and its consequences.
6. Who else has consequences for your choices?

❋ THOUGHTS, FEELINGS, AND ACTIONS

1. Name a feeling.
2. Name an action or behavior.
3. What do you think about recess?
4. Name a situation where different people have different thoughts and feelings.
5. What might someone think about math class?

6. Think of something lots of kids don't like. What is something good about that thing?

❈ FRIENDSHIPS

1. Complete the sentence: My friends like it when I...
2. Complete the sentence: My friends don't like it when I . . .
3. Name something your friends do.
4. Name something your friends don't do.
5. Name one thing you could do to make a new friend.
6. Describe friends you have seen on TV, in a movie, or in a book.

❈ FEELINGS

1. When do you feel happy?
2. When do you feel sad?
3. When do you get mad?
4. When do you get excited?
5. When do you feel scared?
6. When do you feel loved?

❈ WORRY

1. How does your face or body look when you are worried?
2. What do you worry about at home?
3. What do you worry about at school?
4. Practice taking three deep breaths.
5. Make all your muscles tight for three seconds. Now relax for three seconds.
6. What is something you can tell yourself to feel better when you're worried?

Recommended Board Games

Labyrinth by Broderbund
Woolly Warriors by Hape

Abducktion by Very Special Games
Jenga (with Any Question)
Candyland by Hasbro (with Any Question)
Hedbanz by SpinMaster Games
Qwirkle by MindWare
Scattergories by Hasbro
Catan by Hasbro
Forbidden Island by Hasbro

Summary

Activities are the fun part of BHIS. I not only provided services to Manuel but also to his little brother. It is fun to hear a kid request an activity because their sibling had so much fun that they talked about it and wanted to do it again. But it's not just fun that brings us to use these activities. Virtues and skills can be strengthened using activities. Use the hidden lessons to reinforce your teaching.

Workbook

Assignment: Pick one of the activities in this chapter. Explain two ways to use it in a session. What need does it fill? How does it help the child's mental health? What problem might it address?

CHAPTER SEVEN

EARLY SESSION TASKS IN BEHAVIORAL THERAPY

Raine

Name: Raine
Age: 13
Gender: Female
Ethnicity: White
School: Oakview School
Health: Good
Family Members: Jane, mother; Bob, stepfather; Lucy, ten-year-old sister; (Bruce) Jr., sixteen-year-old brother; Bruce, father
Relationship: None
Family Health History: Grandmother recently passed after stroke
Alcohol/Drug Use: None
Challenges: Defiance, abuse history, sexual abuse victim
Goals: Better grades, taking responsibility for self, less talking back
Coping Skills: Forgetfulness, isolation
Strengths: Writing, schoolwork
Weaknesses: Defiance toward parents

Symptoms/Problems: Paying attention, hyperactivity, fire setting
Diagnosis: ADHD, depression
Treatment Goals/Progress:
Comply with parental requests 50 percent of the time, up from 30 percent, within six months
Complete personal hygiene tasks daily without reminding within six months
Improve self-esteem as evidenced by listing three strengths without prompting within twelve months

Case Conceptualization and Discussion:

BUILDING RELATIONSHIPS

Raine is a thirteen-year-old girl growing up but not as fast as Mom would like. She lives with her mother, stepfather, younger sister, and older brother. They live in a low-rent home whose upkeep is suspect. Often, appliances or the car break down, leaving the family in difficult circumstances. Raine's father lives nearby, but his home is not safe for the children due to maintenance problems. In addition, Raine refuses to speak to him due to her perception of his lack of attention. Her brother is violent and has spent time in treatment for abusing her and her sister, and her stepmother is on the sex offender registry for abusing Raine. Her father has also displayed abusive tendencies toward her brother.

Raine is depressed or angry in turn. While generally immature, Raine has more experience in many areas than her peers, leading to a mismatch. Raine prefers to make friends with younger children whom she can control. She is not ready to discuss her abuse or deal with its effects.

In therapy, Raine spends most of her time processing her frustrations with peers and family members. She benefits from expressing herself without having to function within the constrictions of polite society. Sometimes she yells or swears to get past her feelings as she begins to manage them.

Enter by the narrow gate. For the gate is wide and the way is easy that leads to destruction, and those who enter by it are many. For the gate is narrow and the way is hard that leads to life, and those who find it are few. (MATTHEW 7:13-14)

Many times, we are afraid of anger and its signs. Children with traumatic backgrounds and those with mental health issues can turn to anger to push people away as protection. A church that loves them through the nastiness of negative emotions can make a huge impact. Raine needs to get past her anger before she can make progress on her other issues. Just as Raine needs to address one issue before she can start on others, tasks need to be taken at the beginning of therapy services.

Early Session Tasks in Behavioral Counseling

So far, we have been talking about how to run an average session. Some tasks can set you up for success, though, and they should be part of the first two sessions. Your goals for the initial sessions should be:

Establish the goals the family/individual wants to work on:
What activities do they enjoy as a family/individual?
What are the current house rules?
What new rules would the family like to implement?
Are the rules posted anywhere or otherwise codified?
What are the current rewards for compliance?
What are the consequences for non-compliance?
Is the family open to modifying the current system?

Complete a Wellness Recovery Action Plan (WRAP) for your sessions. The WRAP is an easy way to tell if you are making progress toward your goals. Included in the appendix are a kid's WRAP and one for youth. These visual representations of the elements of a WRAP are easier for kids.

❃ SETTING GOALS

What is a goal? That sounds like an easy question, but we look for specific things in a goal.

❃ SMART GOALS:

SMART stands for:

Specific: What should happen to whom? (Client will decrease the number of outbursts)
Measurable: Identify baseline and change expected (Decrease from ten per week to three per week)
Attainable: Based on progress rather than cure (Decrease, not eliminate)
Relevant: Logically related to overall goals (Decrease behavior, not keep client out of trouble)
Timely: Limited in time and space (Within the next ninety days, while in school)

Setting Appropriate Goals for BHIS Services

Behavioral modification, or the use of rewards and punishments to reduce problematic behaviors, should be combined with teaching children to respond differently to situations that cause them trouble. These plans can give us the path toward better behavior and fewer problems for the children.

❃ COMPLIANCE

Behavioral issues are often accompanied by difficulty with following rules, both at school and at home. Teaching a child to follow rules is an appropriate use of time in BHIS programs. In working on compliance, consider any biological, environmental, or developmental barriers to following rules, and design your program with these in mind.

ANGER MANAGEMENT

Difficulty in managing anger is a common reason for referral to a BHIS program. Note that we strive to manage anger, not stop it. Anger is natural. Responses to it can be trained. Children with difficulty managing their anger may find themselves in fights or have explosive temper tantrums. Children can be taught alternative ways to respond to their anger, such as replacement activities or deep breathing.

COPING SKILLS

The objective of BHIS services for children almost always includes coping skills. Parents, teachers, and other important adults, mostly subconsciously, model coping skills for children. Some children need different role models or more overt teaching of these skills. By using commonly experienced conflicts and disappointments, BHIS providers can give children the tools to cope more effectively. When children know better, they do better.

CONFLICT RESOLUTION

Children with behavioral health concerns often have difficulty resolving conflicts with peers, family members, and others. They need more advanced skills in this area. Resolving conflicts can lead to more regulated behavior and more happiness as they get along better with family and make new friends.

Those who start well are half done. Some tasks should be done in the first two sessions as they lay the groundwork for subsequent work. Proper planning prevents poor performance, they say. Laying a good foundation with proper goals sets kids and our program up for success. With Raine, sessions could go off on a tangent without focusing on a specific goal.

Workbook

Joey throws temper tantrums every day that last for an hour. Write a SMART goal for him.

____
____
____
____
____
____
____
____
____
____
____
____
____
____

CHAPTER EIGHT

COPING SKILLS AND BARRIERS

Moira

Name: Moira
Age: 16
Gender: Female
Ethnicity: Black
School: Blackstone School
Health: Good
Family Members: Stephanie, mom
Relationship: Jon, seventeen-year-old boyfriend
Family Health History: Mom, borderline personality disorder
Alcohol/Drug Use: Underage drinker
Challenges: Single parent with borderline personality disorder (often suicidal); difficulty with emotional regulation
Goals: Improve relationship with Mom, exercise emotional management
Coping Skills: Cutting, smoking
Strengths: Compassion, good grades
Weaknesses: Lack of emotional control, attention-seeking
Symptoms/Problems: Emotional regulation
Diagnosis: Disruptive mood dysregulation
Treatment Goals/Progress:
Gain emotional control as evidenced by 10 percent fewer outbursts per week by six months

Refrain from illegal or risky activities from three times per week to one time per week

Improve relationship with Mom as evidenced by reduction in frequency of fights from three times per week to one time per week

Case Conceptualization/Discussion:

EMOTIONAL REGULATION

Moira was a sixteen-year-old "wild child." This young woman was all over the place emotionally. As my mother used to say, when she was good, she was very good, and when she was bad, she was horrid. Moira lived with her mother in a nice rental property. Moira's mom admitted that she had been diagnosed with borderline personality disorder, and Moira's emotions were not the only ones that were extreme.

It did not matter what the emotion; Moira experienced it in the extreme. Her happiness made her take risks. She drove after drinking. She smoked. Her sadness led her to engage in self-harm. Moira has no suicidal impulses but said she cut because that produced pain she could control. She also learned by watching her mother that threats of suicide led people to pay her more attention.

Moira is learning about her mother's diagnosis and more positive reactions. She has been referred to her physician for medication management and taught coping skills outside of self-harm. Self-harm is not always a cry for help or a sign of suicidal ideation. In Moira's case, it is a coping skill or a means of coping with overwhelming emotions. Just like smoking, self-harm can be a coping skill, though not a positive one.

Coping Skills and Barriers

Coping strategies are techniques that help reduce negative feelings when feeling stressed. Those feelings might be the result of anxiety, anger, depression, or general day-to-day stress. Practicing coping strategies can help kids and young adults learn how to manage their emotions in a positive way.

Every child or young adult should have a toolbox of coping strategies that work for them. It is important to recognize that what works for one person may not work well for another. For example, one student may utilize a stress ball quietly and calmly to reduce anxious feelings during a test. A different student may try to use that stress ball and find themselves unable to hold onto it without tossing it, only creating more anxiety about getting in trouble. It is important to have a large list of positive coping strategies from which kids and young adults can choose.

Coping strategies fall into four categories: physical management, emotional management, social management, and negative techniques. Physical management includes techniques for responding physically to stress, such as exercise and breathing techniques. Emotional management includes techniques to deal with the emotional effects, such as meditation and mindfulness. Social management utilizes other people to help maintain equilibrium. An example of a negative technique for adults would be smoking to reduce social anxiety.

Barriers to Therapy Progress

While coping skills enhance mental health, barriers stand in the way of healthy responses to mental health challenges. Some arise within the individual while others are external, like family circumstances. Common barriers include:

Fear
Unclear communication between a therapist and client
Severe symptoms
Substance use
Distractions
Dissatisfaction or disinterest
Inability to listen to others

Lack of trust and transparency
Differing communication styles
Conflict in the home
Cultural and/or language barriers
School conflicts
Sometimes, no matter how many coping skills a person has, they cannot choose better behaviors. As a provider, do not take it personally.

Teaching Coping Skills

Coping skills are techniques to help children and young adults manage tough situations and emotions. Simply providing a list of ideas is not enough. We have to teach kids how to use the skills. For our clients to effectively use these skills, they must be taught, and those skills must be practiced. Practice is essential. If these techniques are put into practice when needed and not just referenced, they must be memorized. They do not need to memorize a list of one hundred, but they need to know how to do it when needed. That means not only learning the strategy but also seeing how it helps. It does not help to write a letter (#35 on the 100 Coping Strategies, link below) if that letter is angry in tone. Show how writing a letter can be a way to express their emotions on the safety of paper. Explore in the letter what makes them angry and positive ways to express it. They must practice asking for a break (#100 on the 100 Coping Strategies, link below) in a low-energy situation, so they can do it when a lot of energy is behind the emotion. Do not wait for the explosion. Role-play it when the child is calm. Here are some coping skills:

1. Take deep breaths
2. Do a positive activity
3. Play sports
4. Think of something funny
5. Take a quick walk

For the full list of the 100 Coping Strategies for emotional management, you can visit https://www.thepathway2success.com/100-coping-strategies-for-anger-anxiety-and-more/.

For more information or additional ideas, you can visit https://thepathway2success.com/coping-strategies-resources.

Many coping skills are primarily distractions. Others engage the muscles in ways shown to have a positive effect, such as cross-body movement. Still others promote pro-social activities and encouragement for connection with others.

Children are not the only ones who will benefit from coping skills. Sometimes you may teach, but the children do not learn. To be successful in teaching coping skills, you need to stay emotionally connected to the child. That connection is foundational to the desire to learn. The rule of thumb is that they do not care how much you know until they know how much you care. Repeatedly in the BHIS program, you will find that a personal connection is the most important aspect of the job. It is not always easy, but it is always worth it.

Involve the senses in the learning process. Activities that engage sight, sound, smell, taste, and touch are the most effective because they are the most memorable. Imagine teaching the concept of working together by making a meal together. All the senses are involved. Use that to build that feeling of teamwork.

Use positive self-talk. Do not allow the children to get down by telling themselves they cannot do it or are not good at it. Find and praise the positive. If possible, you are better off ignoring the negatives than focusing on them.

Acknowledge your emotions instead of trying to hide them. Help your clients to do the same. This involves identifying physical sensations related to the emotion. Does your face get hot when you are angry? Does your throat choke up when you are sad? Label the emotion, then manage the emotion. Talk about it. Use the metaphor of Mentos in a Coke bottle. The explosion is worse when you try to stop it. That's what happens when you don't talk about your feelings.

Prioritize self-care. Try relaxation techniques or guided meditation. You can find clips on YouTube. Do something nice for yourself when your responsibilities are frustrating. Not only can you use these techniques, but you can teach the children to use them.

Moira has fallen victim to negative coping skills in the past, including cutting, smoking, and other risky activities. In part, she has learned these coping skills from her mother, who also uses negative coping skills. A church's role is not limited to teaching, but can also provide role models in people who experience problems but can model better skills. Imagine the youth leader going through a divorce who begins going on mission trips with their extra free time.

Workbook

Find two coping skills for each category:

A) Physical Management
B) Emotional Management
C) Social Management

CHAPTER NINE

FAMILY SESSIONS

Johnny

Name: Johnny
Age: 5
Gender: Male
Ethnicity: White
School: JKL School
Health: Underweight
Family Members: Becky, mom; Jack, grandpa
Relationship: None
Family Health History: Grandpa, bladder cancer; Mom, mental health issues
Alcohol/Drug Use: None
Challenges: Focus, discipline, defiance
Goals: Obey adults, sleep hygiene, focus
Coping Skills: Tantrums, biting, violence
Strengths: Loves cars, sense of humor
Weaknesses: Defiance, irregular schedule
Symptoms/Problems: Defiance, violence
Diagnosis: Oppositional Defiant Disorder
Treatment Goals/Progress:
Comply with adult directives from three times per week to six times per week

Practice good sleep hygiene with a specific bedtime each night, from no nights per week to three nights per week

Utilize positive coping skills from once per week to four times per week

Case Conceptualization and Discussion:

❃ CONSISTENCY

Johnny is a five-year-old boy who lives with his mother in Grandpa's rental property. He often soils himself when upset. He refuses to eat with the family but fills up on junk food after they go to bed. He spends most of his time on screens when he is not at school. He becomes violent when given directions, hitting, kicking, and biting his mother. Mom has recently divorced her husband after six months of marriage and three years of dating.

Johnny shows no ability to self-regulate, but other than refusing to do seatwork, he has no issues at school. His violence toward his mother has left physical evidence on her body. He once broke her finger by bending it backward. As he grows, she is in danger of greater damage. Discipline is erratic, and there is no routine at home. Johnny is dragged along wherever Mom goes at night. There is no set bedtime, and supper is often fast food in the car. Johnny's prime male role model was his stepfather, who is no longer in his life.

Johnny needs a realistic schedule for a five-year-old. His counselor tries to instruct Mom in this need and help her establish such a schedule. She teaches Johnny anger management skills and teaches Mom ways to recognize Johnny's anger before he explodes. She encourages Mom to stop taking Johnny everywhere with her so that he can develop some natural independence. She also stresses to Mom the importance of a regular bedtime and sleep hygiene or having a routine.

Family Sessions

Children are not the only BHIS clients. Their families are also clients in need of services. Sometimes a parent's lack of skills exacerbates their child's needs. Sometimes the child's needs overwhelm the family. Often, multiple children in a family all need individual services as well as services as a family. The interactions between siblings or between children and parents can also be a focus for services.

As a guideline, family services should be provided at a rate at least half that of individual services times the number of children. Two children receive one hour of services each. The family unit receives one hour of services. Four children receive one hour of services, and the family receives two hours of services. Four children should receive one hour times one-half, equaling two hours.

Many tasks for initial sessions (see Chapter 7) can and should be done with the family as a whole or the parents and one child. This is a family session. Current and desired family rules should be a full family topic of discussion in which the parents and children can work together to make a short list of rules and put them on display posters. Parents and individual children can work together on the goals for the child's sessions.

Much of family therapy may be primarily about the family working together. Promoting this and assisting them in making it happen is key. That may mean playing games together as a family. It may be working together to make a family meal. Maybe it is working on an art project together. Often, the family sessions are held in the home, allowing the BHIS provider to observe any health or safety concerns and allowing the family to have a safe and comforting environment in which to work.

TRIANGULATION

One area to watch in family sessions is triangulation—manipulating a person by forming a coalition with another member of the larger group through threats of exclusion. It occurs when communication between two individuals is limited to communication through a third. Imagine the age-old situation of, "Well, Dad said I could!"

UNREALISTIC EXPECTATIONS

Parents are not experts in child development and may expect too much or too little of their children. They may have the same expectations of children of different maturity levels. It may be important to model and teach what can and cannot be expected of the children in a family.

CHILD ABUSE

Parents are unlikely to abuse their children in front of a provider, but you may be in a position to hear explanations for injuries that do not match the parents' explanations or do not fit the circumstances given by the children. Be aware of your program's procedures for reporting child abuse and remember that as a provider, the ultimate responsibility for reporting lies with you.

Family Activities

Many activities in this book can also be done by a family, but below and on the next page are some specific to family sessions. It is important to include family activities to reinforce bonds between family members. Activities might also allow you to observe interactions you would not otherwise see or hear about. Here are some ideas for family activities:

- Family Portrait: Collaborate as a family in drawing a portrait of each member of the family on a piece of paper. As the provider, watch placement of members, size of figures, anything that distinguishes them from one another. Who draws and who instructs or is not involved?

- Family Zoo: Bring a selection of animal toys and have the family work together to choose an animal to represent each person. Talk about why that animal was chosen. Who was the main decision driver?
- Teamwork: Split into two teams for any game. Note who is on each team. Who oversees organizing this activity? Who sits back and watches? Do parents take charge? Is it boys versus girls?
- Family Sculpture: Have one person place family members in a tableau that shows how they respond to conflict. The person then explains why they constructed it that way. Next, a different person rearranges the scene and explains their perspective. Give each person a chance to resculpt and explain.
- Genogram: A genogram is like a family tree, except it uses symbols to explain relationships and can include close, non-family relationships as well.
- Emotions Ball: Write the names of feelings on a beach ball and play catch. When someone catches the ball, they have to talk about a time they felt the emotion that their right thumb lands on.
- Listening to a Biography: Practice active listening (Chapter 5) by having the parent give a biography of themselves or a child.
- The Newlywed Game: Pair up and answer questions about yourself. See if your partner answers the same way. Parents should be paired with children.
- Mirroring: Two family members stand facing each other. One does physical actions or facial expressions while the other mirrors them. Change it up and have the mirror be the initiator.

Family activities can be great relationship builders. They can also reveal a lot about family dynamics that you would have a hard time discovering otherwise. Johnny's family sessions showed his mother had a need to always be in charge, rarely letting Johnny have a say in the activity, even if it was structured to promote shared responsibility. Through coaching, she let Johnny have more of a say in activities without checking out of the process herself.

Workbook

Play a game as a "family." Discuss with your group things you noticed about who took charge and who sat back by themselves. What did you learn about working together?

CHAPTER TEN

DEALING WITH DIFFICULT PARENTS

Abby

Name: Abby
Age: 17
Gender: Female
Ethnicity: White
School: ABC Alternative school
Health: Overweight
Family Members: Paula, mom; Jason, eight-year-old brother; Matt, dad
Relationship: Erin, seventeen-year-old girlfriend
Family Health History: Good
Alcohol/Drug Use: None
Challenges: Child of divorce, depression, anxiety
Goals: Go to college, move out of parental homes
Coping Skills: Eating, music, dancing
Strengths: Relationship-building
Weaknesses: Depressive symptoms
Symptoms/Problems: Difficulty falling asleep, uncontrolled snacking
Diagnosis: Depression, anxiety
Treatment Goals/Progress:
Increase use of positive coping skills from five times per week to eight times per week

Uphold boundaries with parents from three times per week to six times per week

Decrease depressive symptoms by participating in extracurricular activities from once per month to once per week

Case Conceptualization and Discussion:

❃ CHILDREN OF DIVORCE

Abby is a seventeen-year-old girl who splits her time between her mom and dad as they pursue a divorce. Her younger brother joins her in this split. Dad lives on the farm and controls a significant income, which he uses to control Abby as she prepares for college. Mom has a small apartment in the city and struggles financially. Both parents use Abby to try to control the other parent. Mom depends on Abby as a confidant, sharing about her personal life.

Abby struggles with the information shared by Mom. It is difficult to see Dad's side when Mom has told Abby all about her financial and sexual struggles and others. Dad senses Abby's preference for Mom and is withholding money for college, making Abby afraid she will not be able to attend.

Abby needs to set boundaries with her parents and refuse to be their go-between. Therapy helps her process the information her mother gives her. Next year, she will be away from home and will continue to need help dealing with the conflict between her parents. The therapist walks a fine line between showing acceptance of her father's rules and encouraging Abby to be true to herself. Acceptance therapy offers a path through.

Dealing with Difficult Parents

You cannot escape dealing with parents when you are dealing with children. They may be biological parents. They may be stepparents or foster parents. Sometimes they are adoptive parents or even significant others of those parents. No matter their classification, you cannot ignore them or their influence on your client.

Parents can be your greatest asset, or they can be yet another deficit for the child to overcome. Thank God for the good parents. Involve them in their child's program. Give them ideas that they can try at home. Support them, and they may just support you.

Some people will counsel you to set your expectations low. If the parents have proven themselves to be difficult to deal with, this may be good advice to avoid disappointment. Difficult parents may have a bad effect on their child's support workers by fueling feelings of injustice or of impostor syndrome, where a person doubts their abilities. Difficult parents may challenge how you carry out your job. They may pressure you to set aside the rules or to favor their child. Do not give in. Tell them you cannot be emotionally manipulated.

Be direct and assertive when dealing with difficult parents. Use I-statements from Chapter 5. Sometimes you must accept that nothing you do will make them happy, but the following steps can help you come out on top.

BE PROACTIVE

Get a jump on the situation by building a relationship with parents before any problems arise. If parents are already on your side, you can be more effective. This works with good parents as well as with parents with a reputation of being difficult. Start relationships by displaying a friendly, reasonable manner before it is needed.

TAKE PERSPECTIVE

Parents who complain are usually genuine in their feelings that their child has been wronged. While it is easy to be defensive, try to hear their side of the story. Maybe they are frustrated and just need a listening ear. Maybe they have a valid point that you have not seen. Be diplomatic. Be honest. Explain your thoughts on the manner. You may not be able to make them happy, but you have seen their side of the conflict.

Remember that even good, loving parents can cause their children damage without intending to. They pass down fears and prejudices. They struggle with their flaws. They may have impaired judgment. They may be limited by emotional or intellectual handicaps. They may be terrified of the judgment of their families, neighbors, or children. Learn to see difficult parents as human and see their shortcomings as a disability.

BE PREPARED

Parents may come to you screaming and cursing. You must be prepared to handle them without losing your calm. A dysregulated professional will never help a dysregulated parent to calm down. You can always ask them to leave and return when they can discuss the problem calmly, but you need to be prepared if a parent becomes combative. Have a way to communicate with someone in authority or at least another adult. If children are present, take measures immediately to ensure their safety.

You do not always get to work with great parents. Even when they want the best for their children, they may not know better, or they may not care for their children's needs above their own. Abby's parents were divorced, and she had one parent in each camp. Mom did not know any better but was open to learning how to help her daughter. Dad was more concerned with winning the divorce than he was with what was best for Abby. Because of Abby's age, we didn't have long to work with her and her mother before she went off to college. Dad was never willing to take part in family sessions. A church can provide role models when a parent doesn't act as one.

Workbook

Case Study: David is a ten-year-old male with a diagnosis of Autism Spectrum Disorder. After his session last week, Mom insisted that his two sisters receive services also. Mary is a five-year-old female. Mom reports that every weekend, when it is time to go to Dad's, she throws a temper tantrum. She has difficulty sleeping most nights and once awakened, has difficulty returning to sleep. Dad reports none of these symptoms when the kids are at his home. The school has reported that Mary has difficulty concentrating and staying seated. Miriam is a three-year-old female and has been sad since her best friend moved away two weeks ago. She has started talking back to Mom. The girls take part in David's family sessions.

What should you do as David's BHIS provider?

___

___

___

___

___

___

___

___

___

___

CHAPTER ELEVEN

RECORDKEEPING

Evan

Name: Evan
Age: 7
Gender: Male
Ethnicity: Asian
School: White Oak Elementary
Health: Speech impediment
Family Members: Bao, father; Ming, mother; Lily, ten-year-old sister
Relationship: None
Family Health History: Father had a heart attack three years ago; mother has an anxiety diagnosis; paternal grandpa survived a heart attack twelve years ago
Alcohol/Drug Use: None
Challenges: Father is a first-generation immigrant, mother was born in this country; client speaks with a lisp, has low self-esteem, and anxiety
Goals: Feel better about himself, reduce anxious tics
Coping Skills: Playing violin, drinking cold water
Strengths: First chair violin in the Children's Orchestra, loves animals
Weaknesses: Speech impediment, lack of focus

Symptoms/Problems: The client often appears to be ignoring his parents and teachers; he has difficulty staying asleep at night; he complains of aches and pains caused by tense muscles, has crying jags that last thirty minutes at least once a week, and has headaches regularly

Diagnosis: Generalized anxiety disorder, rule out hearing loss

Treatment Goals/Progress:

See audiologist to rule out hearing loss

Learn and implement relaxation skills one time per day from three times per week

Improve compliance with adult directives from three times per day to six times per day

Case Concept and Discussion:

❁ DIFFERENTIAL DIAGNOSIS

Evan is a seven-year-old male, born to Burmese parents. His father came from Burma as an immigrant. His mother was born to immigrant parents. He was referred by his sister's Sunday school teacher.

Evan's mother has self-reported anxiety, and both father and grandpa have suffered from heart attacks. Anxiety is common in his family, but his symptoms may have another cause—hearing loss. It would explain ignoring adults and possibly headaches.

Recordkeeping

The biggest difference between teaching Sunday school or VBS and providing BHIS services may be recordkeeping. Progress notes are a means of standardized communication between providers to convey important information that enables appropriate treatment. If you are charging insurance for sessions, they are also required by that industry to establish medical necessity. Good notes help you to recall details about the case. They minimize confusion and misinformation. A basic form of the progress note is the SOAP note, standing for Subjective, Objective, Assessment, and Plan.

Subjective refers to a neutral retelling, reporting what the client said or did. It may also include information reported by the parents or other individuals involved in the client's treatment. It includes the chief complaint or presenting problem and the history of the problem. Be sure to include details such as frequency, duration, and intensity of the symptom. Include known triggers, cultural factors, and social or contextual factors. It may also include short, sound-bite quotes but not paragraphs. Include client strengths or positive things they see in themselves. Though not required by insurance, these present a fuller picture to other providers reading the notes.

Objective information is that which is measurable. This includes signs of the client's emotional state as well as results from assessments such as the PHQ-9 (Patient Health Questionnaire). If a client reports symptoms, they belong in the subjective section. If the clinician observes symptoms, put them in the objective section.

Assessment is your impression and interpretation of the first two sections. Does the client seem to be improving? Is there the possibility of a differential diagnosis? This section is short, at only one to two sentences.

Plan is the final section. Again, it is short. State how you plan to address the symptoms in the future. Remember: you are addressing symptoms, not diagnoses. Include plans for where and when the next session is planned.

Example SOAP note:

The client reported to BHISP that they continue to have nightmares and wake up, but cannot remember what the dream is about. Her parents state that these happen around twice a week. At the beginning of services, nightmares happened five times a week. The family's culture places great importance on dreams and wants the client to remember the content of her

dreams. The client believes in the importance of dreams and considers dreaming one of her strengths.

During the session, the BHIS provider conducted a biweekly PHQ-9 with the client. (The Patient Health Questionnaire, commonly called the PHQ-9, is a well-respected assessment of a client's mental health, particularly of their experience of depression. You may recognize its use by your doctor's office. It is important to include standard assessments as proof of medical need. The PHQ-9 does not need special training to administer.) Her total score was twenty-three, down from the last time. The biggest decrease was from four to two on thoughts that she would be better off dead. The client reports no suicidal ideation this week. She appears to be improving.

Next week's session will be held at FBC at 4:00 p.m. on October 12, 2024, and will include mindfulness exercises.

If your program is receiving reimbursement from insurance, it will be required of you to keep records that prove medical necessity. You need to work with your licensed provider to ensure medical necessity, but even if this is simply a service you are providing without charge, records are a professional way to ensure that there is continuity of care between providers. Evan's case is an example of the need for records. If we had medical records, we might not need to rule out hearing loss. If a doctor wants to know why we are requesting tests, they might show that reason.

Workbook

Jill is an eight-year-old client who takes atomoxetine (a prescription medicine primarily used to treat ADHD). She has trouble sleeping and is irritable the next day. She complains of having headaches and, when stressed, will often have a tummy ache, even to the point of throwing up. Dad complains of Jill's aggression toward her younger brother. What is your advice to the family?

APPENDIX ONE:

YOUTH WRAP

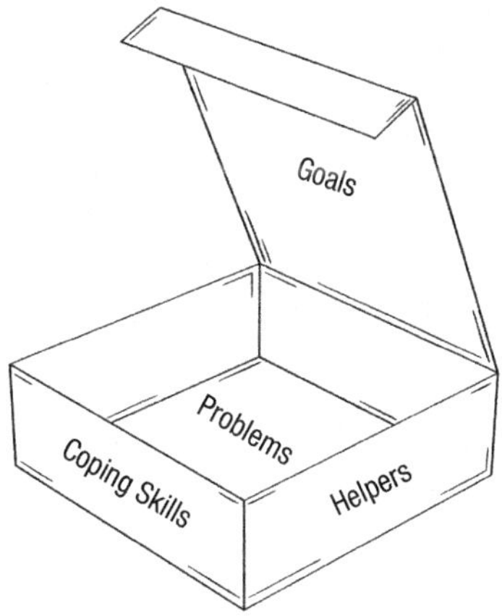

Problems:

Goals:

Helpers:

Coping Skills:

CHILD WRAP

Pie Wrap: Have kids fill out, or scribe them. Use client's words.

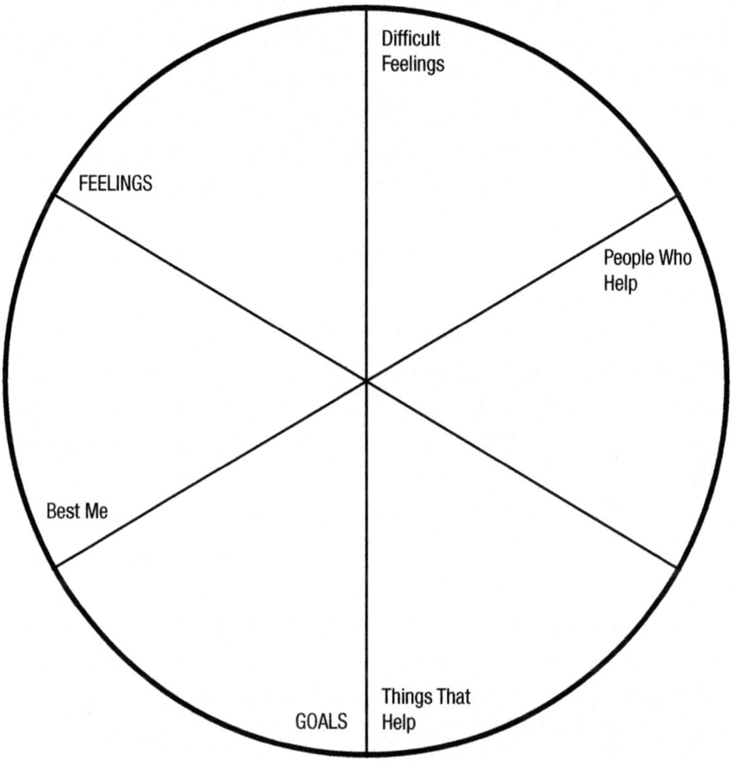

APPENDIX TWO:

FACILITATOR'S GUIDE

Workbook Assignments

❋ INTRODUCTION

Personal questions to be answered with introspective honesty:

1. How did you become interested in BHIS services?
2. What strengths do you bring to this work?
3. What do you need to learn to be an effective BHIS counselor?
4. What experience do you have working with youth from ages three to twenty?

❋ CHAPTER 1

What developmental stage is the client in according to each theorist? Give evidence to support your decision.

Piaget states that the client, as a ten-year-old, is in the concrete operational stage. Erikson would likely place the client in the stage of Industry vs. Inferiority. The client is relying on the teacher to provide rules of play but is trying out the boundaries and pushing the rules to see if they can "get away" with other activities. According to Kohlberg's theory, we could place the client in Level 1, Stage 2. The teacher is the authority figure, but the client is focused on their own self-interest. This is slow moral development for the client's age.

❋ CHAPTER 2

Discuss how the girl's comment made the client feel. Highlight any anxiety. Then discuss her reaction and how it happened. Highlight the connection to anxiety again. Discuss if she wants to repair the friendship and how that could be done.

CHAPTER 3

Role-Play with a Partner. Choose the aggressor in one situation and the victim in the other. The purpose of the role-play is to remind or teach the provider the feelings associated with each role. Afterward, you may choose to debrief providers and ask how they felt, what they noticed, and if they learned anything.

CHAPTER 5

Discuss as a group.

CHAPTER 6

Discuss as a group. Maybe make posters of the affirmation to hang around the house. Make a locker magnet. Write the affirmation ten times. Make a puzzle.

CHAPTER 7

Specific refers to the target behavior. Measurable contains numbers. Attainable means change is not large (two or three). Realistic shows knowledge of Joey. Timely refers to when a goal will be accomplished. For example, "Joey will reduce tantrums by fifteen minutes by next month," or "Joey will reduce tantrums to every two days by the end of the quarter."

CHAPTER 8

Find two coping skills for each category:

- Physical Management
- Emotional Management
- Social Management

Accept reasonable answers. Examples:

Physical: Deep breaths, dance
Emotional: Use positive self-talk, write a thank-you note
Social: Take a time out, talk to an adult

❋ CHAPTER 9

Play a game together as teams. Practice noticing who takes charge, who sits back, and what you can notice about working together.

❋ CHAPTER 10

Case Study: What should you do as David's BHIS provider?

You cannot diagnose. If your program does not require diagnosis, invite them to enroll the younger children. If a diagnosis is required, refer them to a licensed professional.

❋ CHAPTER 11

You cannot recommend a change in medication. You cannot recommend medication. You can discuss medication side effects and suggest that Jill see her medication manager or primary care provider (PCP).